Who Else Is You?

Who Else Is You?

How to Reduce Your Risk of Becoming an Identity Theft Victim

Cindy Schroeter Graham

Published by CSGraham
Battlement Mesa, CO

Published by CSGraham
PO Box 726, Battlement Mesa, CO 81635
WhoElseIsYou@easyas123.biz
www.WhoElseIsYou.com

Care has been taken to ensure that the information in this book was
accurate at the time of publication. Be advised that addresses,
phone numbers, email address, etc., may change and companies
may go out of business or change their products or services. We are
happy to receive corrections, comments and suggestions for future
editions. The reader assumes all responsibility for any actions taken as
a result of anything contained in this book. The author and publisher
shall have neither liability nor responsibility to any person or entity with
respect to any mishaps or damage caused, or alleged to be caused,
directly or indirectly by the information contained in this book.

ISBN 0-9768087-0-6

Printed in the United States of America
10 9 8 7 6 5 4 3 2

Copy editing by Edit et Cetera
Book design by Latentco Design
Graphics by JC Design; jcdesign_1986@yahoo.com

Dedication

This book was made possible by the support
of my loving husband,
the help of a truly great best friend,
inspiration from my sister and my wonderful
mother.

I dedicate this book to Stephen, Hope,
Pam and Edna.

Acknowledgements

People influence us in a variety of ways. Some directly and others do so indirectly. Either way, the influences of the following people have added to the growth and development of the author to enable her to expand her horizons. Those that had an indirect influence may not even be aware of the impact they have had on her life, yet their influence may have been the most important.

One of those people is Michael Koski. Who, in an indirect way, is the one responsible for the path of the author that led to writing this book.

The others include:

Dr. Judith Briles, Mile High Press, for her enthusiasm, guidance and encouragement. (milehighpress.com)

Linda Lane, Edit et Cetera, for her guidance, patience and expertise. (www.familybookhouse.com)

Jeff Herman, The Jeff Herman Agency, for his candor, advice and belief in this book. (jeff@jeffherman.com)

Michael Manley Computer and Telecommunications Services, for his computer expertise. (Michael@mmcats.net)

Jim Corley, State Farm Insurance, for his enthusiasm and input. (Jim.Corley.nyq7@statefarm.com)

Sue Lutz, Dialogue Publishing, Inc., for her patience through all my questions during the CIPA College. (dialoguepublishing.com)

Colorado Independent Publishers Association (CIPA). As a group, CIPA has provided instruction, guidance and encouragement to a "Newbie" that would take years to learn by oneself. (cipabooks.com).

Thank you everyone, for your support.

Cindy Graham

Table of Contents

Introduction

"And our grand prize winner is..."

The emcee reached into the large container and pulled out a small piece of paper. He unfolded it.

"...Cindy Graham!"

The audience applauded wildly.

"Will Cindy Graham come up and claim her prize."

A woman in the third row hastened to the stage.

Another woman from the back hurried forward.

Silence settled over the room.

The emcee looked from one woman to the other. "It seems as though we have TWO Cindy Grahams." He cleared his throat. Then he smiled. "We'll just check drivers' licenses."

Cindy Graham #1 pulled out her driver's license.

Cindy Graham # 2 pulled out her driver's license.

The women glared at each other as they both reached for the check.

"We have a problem. I think we're going to need more identification, ladies," the emcee said with a cough.

Each Cindy Graham offered several pieces of proof of each ones identity.

"This is going to require some research, ladies and gentlemen," the emcee announced with a frown. "I guess we won't have a winner tonight after all."

Identity theft and fraud can touch any one of us with its far-reaching tentacles. No one is immune. While becoming a victim cannot always be prevented, there are several ways to reduce your risk. The information in these pages will help you to minimize *your* chance of having someone else be "you."

Who Else Is You is divided into five sections. The first one contains a survey that examines your current risk levels and discusses how identity theft happens. Section Two offers tips to minimize your risk of becoming a victim. The third section supplies guidance in organizing your information. It will help you monitor your information *before* you become a victim and show you the steps to take if you *do* become a victim.

Section Four provides valuable resources. The fifth section contains action plans, worksheets, and sample letters.

When you complete the worksheets, all your personal information will be in one place, easily accessible to you, along with references and contacts at your fingertips. Once you have entered your information on the worksheets, make sure you put it in a secure place, *out of the reach of would be thieves*.

Responsibility for reducing the risk of identity theft and all efforts involved in the recovery process lie with the reader. This book is not intended to take the place of, or represent, any legal advice or legal documentation that may be required prior to, during, or after fraudulent activity is suspected or confirmed.

The author has provided this information for guidance in protecting against identity theft and fraud, and makes no claims as to the effectiveness of the information herein. Neither the author, nor publisher, shall be held responsible for any losses the readers may incur. The references and contacts are accurate as of the publishing date of this book. The author shall not be responsible for subsequent changes to the information.

Who Else Is You?
How to reduce your risk of becoming an identity theft victim.

Section One:
How At Risk Are You?

At Risk Survey
How Identity Theft Affects You
Identity Theft is Big Business
What is Identity Theft?
How Do Thieves Get Your Information?
How Thieves Use Your Information
A Typical Day

Who Else Is You?
How to reduce your risk of becoming an identity theft victim.

Chapter 1
How At Risk Are You?

To find out your current level of risk, answer the questions in the following survey. Think of what you do normally throughout your day. This should be a realistic review of your daily habits, so choose the answer closest to the way you go about your daily activities. Do not answer the questions the way you *believe* you should be doing things. Only honest answers will give you a true perspective on your current risks of becoming an identity theft victim. You can make changes later that will help reduce those risks, but first let's see where you are today.

Who Else Is You?
How to reduce your risk of becoming an identity theft victim.

At Risk Survey

1. Do you carry you Social Security card with you?
   a. I have it in my wallet or billfold.
   b. Sometimes I carry it—when I think I'll need it.
   c. I never carry it. I keep it in my safe deposit box or a fire proof locked box, and I have memorized the number.

2. Do you keep your purse or wallet secure or in your possession?
   a. Sometimes I put my purse in the grocery cart and turn my back on it. Or, I keep my wallet in my back pocket even in a crowded place.
   b. I try to keep it in my sight at all times, or at my desk at work.
   c. I always keep it in my possession, or locked in a drawer at work

3. Do you pick up your mail regularly or use a locked mailbox?
   a. I leave town and don't make arrangements for my mail to be picked up.
   b. Sometimes I forget to pick up the mail for a couple of days.
   c. I pick up my mail as soon as possible after delivery, or I have a locked mailbox.

4. Do you shred all pre-approved offers and other papers that have your name on it?
    a. I don't have a shredder.
    b. I usually do. I have a single strip shredder.
    c. I cross shred everything that has my name on it.

5. When do you take out your personal trash for pickup?
    a. I take my personal trash to the dumpster any time I need to.
    b. If I have a lot, I will take it out before trash pickup day.
    c. I wait until trash pickup day to take out my personal trash.

6. Do you know the closing date of your statements and the day they should arrive in the mail? (bank, credit card, mortgage, cell phone.)
    a. I don't know when to expect any of my statements.
    b. I know the dates of some, not all, of my statements.
    c. Yes, I know the dates of all my statements.

7. Do you give out personal information over the Internet?
    a. I give out information on a lot of web sites as well as through email links. They look like the real sites, so what's the problem?
    b. I look at the site or link. If it looks secure, I'll go ahead. I also give out my information through links provided in emails if I think they look secure.
    c. I only give it out over secure sites I am familiar with. I never use links provided in emails.

8. When you answer security questions, do you use your Mother's maiden name?
    a. Yes, if they ask for it, I give it.
    b. Only if they don't offer any alternate security questions.

c. No, I made up a different name that I use instead.

9. When you're at an office, if an employee asks for you Social Security number, do you provide it without asking why?
   a. Yes, if someone asks for it, I tell him/her. They must need it.
   b. I only tell it to people in places I am familiar with, like the doctor's office.
   c. If it is an office where I know the procedures for using my SSN, I will write it down and hand it to them.

10. Do you keep your PIN or passwords written down and handy?
    a. My PIN is on my ATM card, or my passwords are taped to the side of my computer or in my desk drawer.
    b. I write them down and try to find a place to hide them that is easy for me to access. I change them a lot so I have to write them down.
    c. I memorize all my PINs and passwords. I write them down and keep them in a secure place.

11. Do you change your passwords regularly?
    a. I use the same passwords, or, if I change them, I just add a number, i.e.., MyDog, MyDog1, MyDog2.
    b. I change it when I think I need to.
    c. I change my passwords regularly.

12. Is your password a name or date related to your family?
    a. I use family names because they are easy to remember.
    b. I use other things I can remember, like my address, birth date, or the last four digits of my SSN.
    c. I use a mix of letters and numbers.

13. Do you know what's on your credit report?
    a. No, not really. I just assume that only my current debts are on the report.
    b. I sort of know. Last time I got a loan the banker reviewed it with me.
    c. I review my credit report every three or four months.

14. Do you leave your checks and/or statements lying around your home or on your desk at the office?
    a. I leave statements or checks out on my desk. My home is safe.
    b. No, I keep my checks in a desk drawer and statements in a file. They are out of sight, but not locked.
    c. I keep checks and statements in a locked drawer or safe.

15. Do you throw away empty prescription medicine bottles?
    a. Yes, when they are empty, I throw them in the trash.
    b. I throw them away only on trash pick up day.
    c. I peel the label off before I throw away the bottle.

16. Do you click on links provided in emails from unknown sources?
    a. Yes. They are convenient to use.
    b. Sometimes, if the link looks legitimate.
    c. Never, I use links I have book marked or I type it in.

17 Do you review your monthly statements for unauthorized activity?
    a. I look at the balance and if it looks about right, I figure there's nothing to worry about.
    b. I review my credit card and bank statements, but none of the rest of my statements.
    c. I review each statement when it arrives. I compare receipts against charges or checks I've written.

18. Do you use virus/firewall/spam/ popup protection?
    a. I have virus protection, but haven't updated it for a while.
    b. I have virus/firewall/spam/popup protection and update it once a month.
    c. I have all the protection and update it on a daily basis, or automatically.

19. Do you review your annual statement from the Social Security Administration?
    a. What is the Social Security Administration annual statement?
    b. I glance over it when it arrives. I look at the retirement part.
    c. I compare the income reported with the income I make.

20. What do you do with your paycheck stub?
    a. I sometimes open it and review it, but I always leave it on my desk.
    b. I put it in my desk and then take it home to review. I put it on my desk at home.
    c. I keep it with me until I get home to review it. Then I put it in a secure place with all the others.

Total your answers.

Use the list below to figure your score. List how many of each answer you have next to A, B or C. Then multiply the total of each category by the points listed with each answer. Add up all your points for your total score.

_____ A answers.

_____ Give yourself 1 point for each A answer

_____ B answers.

_____ Give yourself 2 points for each B answer

_____ C answers.

_____ Give yourself 5 points for each C answer

_____ Total your score

How do you rate?

Compare your score with the categories below to determine your current level of risk.

20-30 Identity theft is a big risk. By changing your daily habits and monitoring your account information, you can reduce your risk of becoming a victim. Start making changes today. Beginning with the basics, work your way into a habit of watching out for those pesky identity thieves every day.

31-40 You are probably aware of the risks of identity theft, but you should take a more pro-active approach. Remember, most reported victims are hit by low-tech means. We can all do something to improve our daily habits and reduce our risks.

41-70 You're doing very well! Nonetheless, there's room for improvement. Look for ways to make changes and to safeguard your information.

71-100 Great job! You are very aware of how your daily habits could result in your personal information getting into the wrong hands. Keep up the good work. More and more people are becoming victims of identity theft every day. So don't slack on your good habits.

If you need to implement some changes to lower your risk, concentrate on making *daily* modifications, working on your weakest areas first. Make changes a daily habit. Some of these may involve the monitoring of your monthly statements. To help you in this, a Monthly Statement Monitoring guide is included in the Action Plan section. Use this form and the Prevention Activity Chart to help organize your account information. This is the great step towards keeping yourself aware of your account activity.

Routine habits, such as giving out your information and the way you handle your daily affairs, may need altering as well. In fact, this may take some extra effort and attention. We are not used to being so protective of our information. We want to trust people. But the times we are living in don't allow us to trust everyone or every business anymore. It's up to you to *want* to protect yourself from becoming an identity theft or fraud victim. Modify your daily habits, and make reminders to keep taking the proper steps to protect your information. It's a lifestyle change that may not come easily, but it will be well worth the effort.

Re-take the test after three months to see if you are consistently making the changes necessary. When you re-take it, make sure you give honest answers pertaining to your new activities. Are you really doing things consistently? If you start to make changes but became lackadaisical after a few weeks, you will reap few benefits. Repeat the test every three months to make sure you are staying on track to reduce your risks of becoming an identity theft victim.

Top Ten
Major Metropolitan Areas
Reported Identity Theft
related complaints.

1. Phoenix-Mesa-Scottsdale, AZ
2. Riverside-San Bernardino-Ontario, CA
3. Las Vegas-Paradise, NV
4. Dallas-Forth Worth-Arlington, TX
5. Houston-Baytown-Sugar Land, TX
6. Los Angeles-Long Beach-Santa Ana, CA
7. Miami-Fort Lauderdale-Miami Beach, FL
8. San Antonio, TX
9. San Francisco-Oakland-Fremont, CA
10. San Diego-Carlsbad-San Marcos, CA

National and State Trends in Fraud & Identity Theft
January -December 2004. FTC Feb. 1, 2005

Who Else Is You?
How to reduce your risk of becoming an identity theft victim.

Chapter 2
How Identity Theft Affects You

There was a time when a handshake closed a deal. Our "yes" meant "yes" and our "no" meant "no." We left our homes unlocked and our children with a neighbor. Trust was commonplace. It was inconceivable during that time to think that someone would violate our privacy, our home, or our children.

Yet, with each passing decade, we are forced to adjust the way we live our lives based on the changing threats and techniques of the criminal mind. We can no longer leave our homes or vehicles unlocked. We need an attorney to review mounds of documentation in order to complete a single transaction. We undergo background checks and lengthy security lines. As long as criminals exist, however, this pattern will never change. With each new act of deception, we must adapt our lifestyles to lessen our chances of becoming victims and reduce the impact these culprits make on our lives.

Criminal minds of past decades have created a species of crooks known as identity thieves. Now, as we go about our usual business each day, these criminals use our willingness to share our personal and financial information against us. We trust that our information will be safe, secure, and kept only in the hands of honest people. Times have changed. A once honest employee may be willing to give out, or sell, confidential information when bribed by a cunning criminal.

The Federal Trade Commission reports that one in eight U.S. adults are affected by identity theft.

Identity Theft Resource Center 2003 report "Identity Theft: The Aftermath"

The recent surge in identity theft crimes has caused us once again to pay closer attention to our activities. We must change the way we casually go about our daily business and the way we pass along our information if we want to fight against identity thieves. We can no longer trust that our information is secure, not at our local market or with a national business. We may feel it is inconvenient to take the initiative, but it is a necessary evil in our daily routines. We must become proactive, changing our habits today to protect our financial futures tomorrow.

We may not like the idea of paying the extra expense for protection, but it, too, is necessary at this time. We already pay for protection with all sorts of other insurance. Does the insurance we have protect us from bad things happening? No. Insurance protects us from the financial devastation caused by the bad things that happen.

Identity theft cannot be prevented. Just like getting hit by a car, it cannot always be prevented. If the other car is going to hit you, it will. So it is with identity theft. It can happen to us no matter what we do. So beware of any company that says it will prevent identity theft from happening to you. We can only reduce our risk of becoming victims. To lessen our chances of being hit by another car, we can avoid a busy highway. Similarly, we can monitor our credit, be aware of how identity thieves get our information, and take steps to reduce our exposure. This way we *minimize* our risk of being hit by an identity thief.

Think all identity thieves are strangers? Think again. Half of all known identity thieves are someone we know or currently do business with. Most people fail to realize they are at a higher risk of becoming victims from someone they know, so they are lax with their information, leaving it unlocked or out on a desk. We are willing to give out our information to people who "sound" like they are legitimate.

Reports show that theft committed by this group (people we know) result in greater total costs and greater out-of-pocket expense and require more time to resolve than frauds committed by strangers. It's not a pleasant thought to consider that, right now, someone you know might be an identity thief or could easily be persuaded to give out information that could result in fraudulent activities. Think about it: A day care provider, nanny, housekeeper, service or repair person, family member, or friend all have access to you and some type of information that is uniquely yours.

> Family, relatives, friends and neighbors make up 50% of known identity thieves.

The ratios indicate that if you do become a victim, chances are the thief is someone you know or do business with on a regular basis. It may be someone involved in your daily course of life or someone who knows your habits. How many people have access to where you keep private information such as your statements, taxes, checks, etc.?

Unfortunately, knowing the perpetrator creates a difficult situation when it comes time to prosecute the thief. No one wants to learn that a relative, friend, or acquaintance is a criminal. Calling the police to report the crime can be very emotional and can put an enormous strain on the relationship between the victim and friend or family member who is suspected of identity theft or fraud.

> During the twelve months prior to January 2005, 9.3 million Americans became victims.
>
> In the past five years approximately 27 million people have had their identities stolen.
>
> National and State Trends in Fraud & Identity Theft January – December 2004. FTC Feb. 2005

Those who fall victim to any type of identity theft will endure aggravation, frustration, confusion, and feelings of helplessness; and the emotional impact can be devastating. Identity theft victims experience such high stress levels that not only do the victims suffer, but also their families and their jobs. The emotional impact reported by many victims has been compared to that of those who suffer violent crimes such as rape, assault, and battering. This devastating side effect should not be taken lightly. Recovering from such an emotional ordeal doesn't happen overnight. Meanwhile, the length of time involved and the high stress levels take a toll on the victims' well being. Many of them, in fact, seek counseling in an attempt to return to their normal lives and their former financial stability, as well as to regain their peace of mind.

The aftermath of becoming an identity theft or fraud victim can last for many years. Numerous victims have reported that efforts to clear their names have taken twelve or more months, and the effects of the crimes continued to haunt them for years with denied credit or criminal records that never go away. Errors that were supposedly cleared up resurface after a few months to re-ignite the original despair of becoming a victim.

In addition to the trauma of being victimized, many have reported that companies involved in the fraudulent activity, as well as the credit reporting agencies, treat them like the criminal rather than the victim. Furthermore, they often find that the companies do little to help them. They even report being treated as though they are trying to get out of paying a legitimate debt.

> Businesses lost $52.6 billion in identity theft and fraud related crimes.
>
> National and State Trends in Fraud & Identity Theft January -December 2004. FTC Feb. 2005

Victims may have to repeatedly produce evidence or documents defending their case to the companies involved. Thus begins a long, cumbersome, and emotional road that lies ahead for the victims of identity theft or fraud.

The businesses left with the losses usually carry some type of insurance that covers them in these cases. Most of them may choose not to investigate the issue or pursue the criminals because they will not be reimbursed for any losses they incur. It's easier to collect the insurance and continue with business as usual than to invest the manpower and expense necessary to address the problem. This practice may result in higher insurances rates for the business, but that doesn't seem to be an incentive for them to do something positive to help the victim recover from the crime.

Many statements are now produced electronically. This creates no paperwork and no worries about mishandled information. However, it's not for everyone. You must decide what works for you because electronic billing requires you to educate yourself about which online sites are secure. Fraudulent sites mislead many people by mimicking legitimate ones. If you choose electronic services, ask the institution about their security, and make sure your computer has protection from viruses and spy ware.

Businesses can distribute personal information compiled from legitimate sources for other marketing companies. These companies only gather public information, such as county or state records including marriage licenses, property records, building permits, etc. Anything available from your local public records office is available to these companies. Information they gather could even include shopping habits. Did you know our purchasing habits are monitored?

There's no way around it—it's all collected and public information. We are living in a time when information gathering is big business. Because of it, we get information sent to us by companies who want to sell us products or services comparable to our current buying trends or interests

Have you ever wondered why you receive all that unsolicited mail offering home equity loans right after you buy a house? Or offers for auto insurance after you buy a car?

Think about it. After any major purchase or life style change, you usually get offers and specials for related products or services. So far, it's not illegal to collect public information. It is unlawful, though, to use the information to commit fraud.

So why is it so easy for an identity thief? Because we, the honest consumers, want our lives to be simple. We want easy to access our own accounts. We want a quick response to our credit needs, like obtaining a credit card or car loan and even getting a mortgage. We want banking to be easy for us.

How many of us have gotten upset with our local bank because one of the tellers asked us for an ID? Do we respond with - "What! I've banked here for over ten years and now you want me to show you an ID? I've never had to show an ID before."

Because we insist that our own lives be hassle free, thieves are able to utilize the same convenient means we do to access our information. More strict business practices are inevitable if we want future privacy and identity protection. Which would you rather have: easy access and increased identity theft or privacy procedures and reduced incidences of theft and fraud?

Start reducing your risk now by asking the financial institutions and businesses you frequent to implement strict identification and privacy guidelines for you, their customer.

Who Else Is You?
How to reduce your risk of becoming an identity theft victim.

Chapter 3
Identity Theft is Big Business

Identity theft is big business. Criminals continuously seek new ways to take our money and run. They started out holding us up at gunpoint. Now they rob us through the financial avenues and information agencies that are supposed to make our lives run smoother and make doing business a little easier.

The crime of identity theft and fraud often takes place behind the scenes. Hidden from view, the thieves hit with a vengeance and disappear. We, the victims, are left to sort through the false information and negative reports and *then* face the long, hard road to recovery. Criminals see identity theft as a low risk, high profit crime. It's low risk because it is easy for them to obtain our information and access our accounts or establish new ones in our names. And few of these criminals actually get caught. It's highly profitable because they can make a quick and significant monetary gain. In other words, they laugh all the way to the bank.

Thieves tend to lapse back into their previous pattern of behavior, especially if it's a pattern of criminal habits. They also have a tendency to repeat the crimes they know. Identity thieves, in particular, believe their "trade" to be "easy street," and they will return to it even after being caught and serving a sentence. It's their comfort zone. Career criminals act as though they believe the money they can steal is a fair trade-off for the relatively short prison term they *might* have to serve.

Another reason identity theft often goes unpunished is the difficulty encountered in identifying and prosecuting the criminal. Most thieves use the stolen information for only a brief time, perhaps just a matter of hours. They get what they can; then they are gone. Unless someone catches the criminal *using* the information—red-handed, as the saying goes—there is little chance of an arrest. Few victims have taken on the daunting task of pursuing their perpetrators, and police officers are already overburdened and may consider physically violent crimes to be more important. Further, they may not want to take the time to work with theft/fraud victims or to investigate a crime that often cannot be solved.

No one will disagree that some of the statistics regarding identity theft and fraud are staggering. Even though we may think we understand all the issues involved or the money that is lost or the time that is spent, we will find the numbers in black and white to be real eye openers. This is, perhaps, the real value of these statistics, for without them we might tend to forget the enormous impact identity theft can have. It affects all our lives, not just those of its victims. So it is vitally important that we realize how frequently it happens, how much it costs, and how easy it is for thieves to get away with it.

Identity theft crimes are not always categorized the same way. Many are listed as fraud complaints and/or fraudulent activity. So it is important that information from all relevant sources be considered when evaluating the magnitude and the impact of this growing crime. Your state may file identity theft cases under other types of criminal activity, such as fraud, fraudulent use of a credit card, forgery, or one of several other categories. Check with your local law enforcement office or your district attorney's office for specifics.

While the statistics on identity theft and fraud would fill a book, focusing on such grim facts will provide no positive benefit. Instead, let's look at what identity theft is, how it happens, and what we can do to reduce our risks of becoming a victim.

"Lodi woman gets 6 months in prison for identity theft"
Lodi Sentinel

Identity theft accomplice gets 42 months
San Antonio Express

A woman serving a 12-year sentence for forgery, theft and fraudulent use of a credit card in Tennessee, plead guilty to leading an identity theft ring. She will cooperate with the prosecution of eight co-defendants. She and the co-defendants were charged with using stolen Social Security numbers and other personal information to steal credit accounts of individuals at department stores.

She was allowed to work in a prison jobs program where she typed in personal information into a state computer. Officials say they will no longer use inmates with a record of financial crimes for this type of work.

February 23, 2004
Memphis Tennessee

Chapter 4
What is Identity Theft?

Identity theft occurs when someone uses your name or personal information, such as your Social Security number, driver's license number, telephone number, cell phone ID, credit card or any other account numbers, without your permission. Congress passed the Identity Theft and Assumption Deterrence Act which prohibits:

> Knowingly transfer[ing] or us[ing], without lawful authority, a means of identification of another person with the intent to commit, or to aid or abet, any unlawful activity that constitutes a violation of Federal Law, or that constitutes a felony under any applicable State or local law. 18 U.S.C § 1028(a)(7)

There are three basic forms of identity theft: financial, cloning, and criminal. The most well known of these is financial theft, crimes related to the use of your personal information to financially benefit someone else. Any type of identity theft or fraud can cause huge problems that plague the victim for years. In many cases, he victims are unaware of any fraudulent activity until they are informed in a negative manner, such as denied credit or being contacted by a collection agency. It's bad enough to fall victim to identity theft and fraud, and even worse to find out when you least expect it or have need of the good credit rating you have spent years building. That's why it is so important to become pro-active in your efforts to lessen your risk of becoming a victim.

> **Identity theft comes in three basic forms:**
>
> **Financial**
> **Cloning**
> **Criminal**

Financial Identity Theft

With your information, thieves can purchase merchandise, as well as apply for loans or mortgages, credit cards, and services like cell phones and utilities. The list is potentially endless. This type of fraud/theft affects your credit scores and thus your ability to obtain credit. Even if the incorrect information is cleaned from your report, you may still be denied credit or have reduced credit scores, which results in your paying higher interest rates long after the original incident.

We hear a lot of stories in the news about this type of theft. Here are some typical scenarios.

You use your credit card for a purchase, and the transaction is declined for no apparent reason. How embarrassing! Even worse, it happens in front of people you know.

You go into a department store. When you check out, you decide to apply for the store's credit card. You have worked hard to maintain your good credit and are confident that you will be approved. However, you are denied. What a shock! You are embarrassed and confused as to why you have been refused.

You decide to purchase or refinance your home. The banker tells you that you have too many outstanding debts, and these must be paid off before you can get the loan. Or you are told he/she can do the loan, but the interest will be four or more points over the average because of your poor credit rating.

Identity Cloning

Another form of identity theft is identity cloning. Someone assumes your name and personal information to, in effect, become *you*. They apply for jobs, rent an apartment, submit insurance claims, file tax returns, or apply for unemployment or welfare. They can use your name to be admitted into the hospital or other health care services. There are even reported cases where thieves have claimed bankruptcy under their victims' names and Social Security numbers. In fact, *anything* you can do, they can now do.

You may not think it's a big deal for another person to become you, but when someone else uses your name and Social Security number, it can be a *very* big deal. Imitation has been characterized as the most sincere form of flattery, but that is NOT always the case. If another person obtains employment using your Social Security number, they begin reporting income to the Internal Revenue Service under that number. YOU will owe taxes on it! Of course, you won't include the income from the "other you" when you file your taxes because you don't even know it's there. Under reporting income can trigger IRS nightmares you don't want to happen. Or the imposter could file an income tax return under your Social Security number and receive a refund. Then, when you file your tax returns, you could be denied your refund because you've already received one!

If the criminal uses your information to get health care, the results can be reported on your health records maintained by the Medical Information Bureau. This could trigger higher insurance rates, or you could even be denied life or health insurance.

In one case, the stunned victim was contacted by authorities for non-payment of child support. How could that be? The perpetrator had been posing as that person for years—entering relationships, producing children, and owing unpaid child support.

Criminal Identity Theft

A criminal can use your driver's license, state identification, or other identifying information when he/she commits a crime. Therefore, all warrants are issued for *your* arrest. Once you are in the police files as being an alias or having a criminal record, that information may never go away. Even if you prove it wasn't you, your *name* remains linked as an alias for the criminal. This can haunt you for the rest of your life. Law enforcement agents do a great job, but if they pull you over, they don't know whether they are stopping the criminal or you. Until you have a chance to produce evidence to the contrary, you *are* the wanted person they believe they have apprehended. Can you imagine anything worse than being an innocent victim and having a police officer draw a gun and demand that restraints be used on you? What a helpless feeling! Until you can prove you are innocent, the officers will think otherwise and treat you accordingly. Because some criminals use stories of mistaken identity to try to convince police they are not guilty, the authorities are unlikely to give much credence to your protestations of innocence. They will follow procedures, and you will have to go along, until you can contact your attorney or provide evidence that you are not the criminal they assume you to be.

Incidence of identity theft increased 11-20% between 2001-2002 and 80% between 2002-2003

Identity theft Resource Center 2003
"Identity Theft: The Aftermath"

Who Else Is You?
How to reduce your risk of becoming an identity theft victim.

Chapter 5
How Do Thieves Get Your Information?

Most of us play by the rules provided by the agencies with which we deal: Department of Motor Vehicles, Social Security Administration, medical and insurance offices. For example, we understand that without certain information we cannot obtain a driver's license. But to a criminal there are no boundaries. A perpetrator can and will find ways to subvert the system and obtain what they want.

One law enforcement agent who was interviewed urged that it was best not to reveal exactly where or how thieves can get your vital information. This is not a course on the art of thievery. Therefore, only general information is provided to help you understand how these criminals operate. Specifics are not included. Just bear in mind that a thief *can* get your Social Security number, along with other personal information

Several basic avenues provide relatively easy access to our personal information. Because the majority of thieves use "low tech" means of obtaining this, we need to be aware that the things we do daily and the habits we have might enable a thief to access to our data.

One obvious way thieves get your information is by stealing your wallet or purse. This method provides them with your identification, credit cards, checks, and bank cards.

Another potential avenue you may overlook is your home. If you have paperwork, statements, checks, or other personal information lying around the house or on your desk, it's easy pickings for a thief. Someone struggling with difficult times could succumb to the temptation to steal your information because it's in plain sight.

Thieves can also steal your mail. This is often a great source of information. Typically, it includes your bank and credit card statements, pre-approved credit offers, new checks, and tax information. Anything you receive in the mail could fall into the hands of a thief.

> Only half of all victims say they know how the identity thief obtained their information.
>
> Nearly one quarter of all victims said their information was either lost or stolen.
>
> National and State Trends in Fraud & Identity Theft January – December 2004. FTC Feb. 2005

Utilizing a related tactic, thieves can complete a "change of address form" at the post office, diverting your mail to another location. Then it's delivered right into their hands.

Thieves can gain access to or steal files out of offices where you are a customer, employee, patient, or student. Bribing an employee or hacking into electronic files are two common methods. In some cases laptops have been stolen from businesses. Or these criminals may pose as legitimate representatives of other companies and be given access to information from a business.

Dumpster divers rummage through trash, looking for personal data from any source. They're more than willing to paste together statements if they think they can obtain the information they want.

Thieves also access the data you provide about yourself on the Internet, even setting up scams to entice you to give up your information. This is usually through emails (but can be accomplished by telephone). They pose as legitimate companies, financial services, or government agencies and try to intimidate you into giving them the information they want.

Skimming is a process used to get your ATM or credit card information. A unit mounted on an ATM machine over the access slot where you insert your card records your information. The ATM works normally, so many victims don't realize their information has been stolen. Avoid ATMs that don't look quite right or that have a lot of ads or announcements taped to them.

If you are in a restaurant and pay with a credit card, the wait staff usually takes your card and returns with your receipt. What happens to your card while it's out of your sight? In some cases, your credit card information is written down or copied on a small, portable skimmer and saved for future use. Then your transaction is completed as usual, and you don't even know your card information has been recorded somewhere else.

As for online thieves, phishing and pharming are the current trends. Phishing is a term used to describe devious online crooks that send out various forms of communication, hoping to trick the receiver into giving out personal information. The most common form of phishing is email. Pharming is a more serious concern. Pharming is a hidden program that redirects you to bogus sites that mimic the sites you thought you were going to. This can be very effective because it's so difficult to detect.

Chapter 6
How Thieves Use Your Information

Once they have your information, the thieves use it to get as much as they can as fast as they can. Here is a summary of reported findings by the Federal Trade Commission.

Credit card fraud constitutes the greatest percentage of reported misuses. Fraudulent usage can be found on both existing accounts and on new accounts set up in the victim's name. How does this work?

On your existing accounts, thieves call and pretend to be you. Then they request to change the mailing address on your account. After receiving your information, they run up charges. Since your statements are now being mailed to a different address, it may be awhile before you realize there is a problem.

Thieves can use your name, date of birth, and Social Security number to open new bank accounts. Of course, they use a different address so you don't have any idea the new accounts are open. The banks don't know that the thieves are not you because they use false identification with your name and Social Security number. With the new accounts thieves take as much as they can as quickly as they can. Then they disappear. Since the accounts are in your name and under your Social Security number, the delinquencies/overdrafts are reported against *you*, and *you* are the one the bank will be looking for to collect the bad debts.

Thieves can also open new service accounts, including wireless accounts, telephone accounts, and household utility services such as electricity or cable. Their main objective is to use these accounts without paying for them. Often they may use a false mailing address so they are not bothered with the bills. You, as the victim, aren't even aware of what's happening. But they've used your name and Social Security number, so the collection agencies will start calling you.

Bank fraud is another avenue thieves take to separate victims from their money. By obtaining access to existing bank accounts—using electronic transfers, counterfeit checks, or debit cards—they can quickly deplete all the funds. How does it work? He/she uses your information to open a new bank account and to transfer existing funds to that account. Then the thief writes checks against the new account. If the checks are bad and are reported to a check clearing service, you may not be able to write your own *good* checks. In addition, you could be denied the next time you try to write a check or open an account.

Loan fraud is committed when the thief uses your identification to obtain business or personal loans, auto loans, and/or real estate loans. Typically, a false mailing address is given along with your name and Social Security number. Thieves receive the funds, and you are again left with the debt traceable to you through your name and SSN. Victims often face the burden of dealing with collection agencies while they are being denied the credit they might need to recover from the fraudulent activities of the thief.

You may find out you are a victim when a police officer shows up at your door with a warrant for your arrest. If criminals use your identity during an arrest, the police put your name into their system. If the criminals are released from custody, they usually won't show up for their court date. An arrest warrant is then issued in your name. The police have no way of knowing you are not the offender. You then have the burden of proving your innocence. But you probably won't even know the police want you—until you are on your way to jail.

More appalling is learning that your child has become a victim. Even infants have fallen prey to these perpetrators. Many parents do not know anything is wrong until they open a savings account or college fund account in the child's name. For example, when opening a new account, the parents of a three-month-old, were told that their child already had a history of writing bad checks.

To avoid having your child's credit ruined before he/she can even write, look for these warning signs that someone else could be using your child's information: He or she starts receiving pre-approved credit offers or catalogs or special offer junk mail. Also, if the thief has made a major purchase, your child could receive offers for insurance or to refinance. If you suspect fraudulent activity in your child's name, review the same reports you would review for yourself. You can request these reports on behalf of your child.

How Victim's Information is misused

Credit card fraud	28%
Phone/utility fraud	19%
Bank fraud	18%
Employee related fraud	13%
Government document fraud	8%
Loan fraud	5%
Other	22%
Attempted identity theft	6%

National and State Trends in Fraud & Identity Theft
January -December 2004, FTC Feb 1, 2005

Chapter 7
A Typical Day

Let's put all this information together and apply it to a typical day in the lives of a fictitious couple named John and Jane. John works full-time in an office, and Jane is a stay-at-home mom with a newborn. Since their family has grown, they have decided to apply for a loan to build an addition on the house.

John leaves for work, stopping to put gas in his car and grab a cup of coffee. Those pay-at-the-pump gas stations speed up the process, but John forgets to grab his receipt.

At lunch, he stops to get money from an ATM. The location is busy, and two people wait impatiently in line behind him. He meets a prospective client for lunch and pays the waiter with a credit card.

Jane takes the baby to the doctor's office for a check up. While there, an office worker asks to verify her insurance information and the baby's Social Security number. After the doctor's visit, she goes to the mall to buy some baby clothes. The cashier rings up the sale while on the telephone. Jane hands her credit card to the cashier. The cashier processes the credit card through the terminal as usual and turns briefly away from Jane, holding the credit card and still talking on the phone. The cashier then hands the card back to Jane, completing the transaction.

On the way home Jane drops off their package of financial information with the receptionist at the lender's office.

At the end of the driveway, she picks up the mail from the mailbox. Among the bank and credit card statements there is junk mail and pre-approved credit offers. She glances through them and throws away all the advertisements and offers she doesn't want to review later in the outside trash can. No sense in taking it inside because it will just be taken out again in a few days.

She later receives a phone call from a charity asking for donations. Jane has always cared about those less fortunate and tries to help whenever she can. Today she makes a small donation by credit card.

She opens all the bank statements and bills and glances through them to see if there's anything wrong, then lays it all on the desk in the office. She'll take care of balancing the statements and paying the bills tomorrow.

Late in the afternoon a service person comes to the door to check on the phone lines. A problem has been reported throughout the neighborhood, so it's a courtesy call just to check that the lines are working. Jane lets the service person in. Her baby cries, so she leaves the service person to his work and tends to her son.

John arrives home with some associates to finish up a project from work. He directs them to wait in his office. A few minutes later, he brings in some coffee and snacks.

At the end of the day all is quiet. John and Jane sleep soundly, anticipating the approval of their loan so they can add on a new room for the baby.

A few weeks go by. John stops to get gas on his way to work; his credit card is declined. He tries his ATM card, and it is also declined.

Jane goes to the bank to open a savings account for the baby. She's told that her infant son has been sent to collections for outstanding bad checks. How can that be? He's only six months old! This would have been his first account.

Bewildered, Jane decides to check on the status of their loan. She is told the loan application has been declined due the number of recently opened credit cards, non-payment on outstanding credit cards, and a car loan that has gone to collections.

How could this happen?

Did you catch the little things that increased their exposure?

Let's review them.

John forgot to get his credit card receipt when he bought gas. The next customer to use that gas pump could have noticed it and taken the receipt, which has John's credit card number printed on it. John should have made sure he got his receipt and kept it in a safe place.

John next used an ATM where several people are waiting. He was not aware of the "shoulder surfer" who was watching him enter his account number and his PIN.

At lunch, John's credit card was completely out of his sight. The wait staff could easily have recorded the number.

Jane's mistakes began at the doctor's office when she told the office worker her son's Social Security number. Anyone sitting in the waiting room could have overheard the child's name and Social Security number. How could she have prevented this? She should have written down the information and handed it to the office person. This way, no one else in the waiting room would over hear the information.

While paying for baby clothes, Jane gave her credit card to a cashier that was on the phone. The cashier could easily have repeated the card information to the other person while completing the sales transaction. Remember that her back was to Jane, who should have waited for the cashier to hang up before handing over her credit card.

Jane felt good about donating to the charity. But did she really know who she was talking to on the phone? Without knowing or verifying the charity, Jane shared her credit card information with a total stranger.

Jane threw out her junk mail and pre-approved applications in her outside trash can, making it easy access to a dumpster diver. Jane should have shredded all her pre-approved applications as well as any junk mail with her name on it.

She also allowed the service repairperson inside to check the phone lines. She was not present while he checked the lines in the office because she went out to quiet her crying baby. That person could have easily written down account information from the mail that she had left on the desk.

Before allowing the service person inside, Jane should have gotten the person's name and company he worked for. Then she should have called the company to verify the employee's name and the reason for the service call.

John allowed his associates to wait in his office while he got coffee for them. They each had access to the mail left on John's desk.

All these circumstances can lead to stolen information—even from people we do business with each and every day.

Who Else Is You?
How to reduce your risk of becoming an identity theft victim.

Section Two:
Be Pro-Active

Become Pro-Active
Tips To Minimize Your Risk
Your Daily Life

Top Ten
Identity theft victims by state

1) Arizona
2) Nevada
3) California
4) Texas
5) Colorado
6) Florida
7) New York
8) Washington
9) Oregon
10) Illinois

National and State Trends in Fraud & Identity Theft
January-December 2004, FTC Feb. 1, 2005

Your state may not be listed above but Identity Theft is a problem in all fifty states and over seas. It affects you no matter where you live.

Chapter 8:
Become Pro-Active

Many people think that electronic channels—online scams—cause the majority of "lost" information. They don't realize that identity thieves rob us in a multitude of ways. In fact, *most* personal information is stolen through traditional, low-tech methods. If we delude ourselves into thinking that we are safe from thieves if we don't share our personal data over the Internet, we will actually *increase* our chances of becoming a victim.

We live in the Information Age. This means a lot of information about everything and everyone is floating around out there—if you know where to access it.

It also means we can reduce our risks of becoming a victim. We don't live in a financial bubble, so nothing can guarantee one hundred percent protection against identity theft. However, we can minimize our vulnerability. And should some scheming crook get our information despite our diligent efforts at prevention, we can educate ourselves to recognize the signs of a problem.

We can compare this to having automobile insurance. Auto insurance doesn't keep us from being involved in an accident. What it *does* do is help us with the aftermath if an accident happens. How *can* we maximize our protection? Traffic laws and procedures have been put in place to help reduce the risks. If we choose not to follow these, however, we, by default, place ourselves in the higher-risk category of accidents waiting to happen.

So it is with identity theft and fraud. Following the procedures outlined in this book won't prevent us from ever becoming victims. But if we act responsibly to reduce our risks—to ensure that we have made every effort possible to minimize exposure to these opportunistic thieves—we will be far better equipped to cope with such an eventuality should it ever occur. Statistics show that one out of every eight people becomes a victim of identity theft or fraud. We can take steps to help reduce our risks of falling into that unfortunate group...or we can take our chances.

Begin with little lifestyle changes that make a BIG difference. At first these may seem to be more trouble than they're worth. However, it is in our own best interest to spend the time on the little things with the goal of saving ourselves from the huge devastation and possible financial loss of identity theft and fraud.

Be pro-active! Start *now* to reduce the risks of becoming a victim.

Chapter 9
Tips to Minimize Your Risk

We cannot prevent identity theft from happening, just like we cannot prevent someone from mugging us. We can, however, become less likely targets. Here are a few areas where we can minimize our risks of becoming victims.

These guidelines will raise your awareness of what you are giving or telling people and how much information you really want them to have. The key is to know who you're talking to. If you *initiate* contact with a business, you will probably use a phone number or website from sources you already have, like statements. But if you *receive* a call or email from the company, you don't really know where it came from, who it is from, or whether they really are who they say they are. Don't be intimidated by a caller or an e-mail that demands immediate action or threats. Many times this is a ploy to scare you into giving out information. Intimidation is the gun in your face in our high tech times.

Who Else Is You?
How to reduce your risk of becoming an identity theft victim.

Your Daily Life

Don't give out your personal information. We do this all the time, and we don't even realize it. It goes back to the times when we trusted our neighbors. We'd like to think we can still trust everyone, but we can't. If you don't know the person or don't know how your information will be used, *DON'T GIVE IT OUT!*

Some places where information is often shared without a second thought include sign-in rosters, applications, membership forms, questionnaires, etc. If you must give out your information, only give your name and a contact phone number. *Make sure you know who will be handling the information and why.*

Consider the following scenario.

The phone rings.

"Hello."

"Is this Cindy Graham?"

"Yes, it is."

"This is XYZ Credit Card Company. I'm calling to verify a $2500 charge on your credit card.

Cindy gasps. "Oh, no! I never charged that to my account. You haven't paid it, have you?" Her heart is pounding.

"That's why I'm calling you. The charge raised some red flags, so we wanted to check with you before honoring it. If you'll just verify your card number that ends with 4321, the expiration date, and the three digit code on the back, we can take this off your account as an unauthorized transaction."

"Yes, yes! Just a moment. Let me grab my card so I can give you all that information."

Cindy provides the requested numbers and hangs up the phone after profuse thanks to the caller.

"Whew!" she exclaims aloud. "Am I glad they called! I just avoided a huge bill ...and an even bigger headache trying to get that charge removed from my account!"

Or did she? What confirmation did she receive that she was actually talking to a customer service representative from her credit card company? She did not initiate the call, and chances are very good that no number showed up on her Caller ID. Yet, in her hurry to avoid a supposed unauthorized charge, she gave away information that made her vulnerable to an unscrupulous identity thief.

Never provide personal financial information, including your Social Security number, account numbers or passwords, over the phone or the Internet if you did not initiate the contact. If you made the call, you should know to whom you are talking. If someone called you, you can never really be sure who you are talking to.

Shred all personal information you throw away. This includes pre-approved credit offers you receive through the mail, contest entry forms, old bills and statements, pre-scription information, and employment information. A cross cut shredder is recommended. It will make it more difficult for a thief to glue the pieces back together. *If your name is on it, shred it.*

Many companies have implemented some standard questions to verify user information. These may include your mother's maiden name, where you went to high school, the year you were born, your favorite pet's name, and so forth. Don't use your real answers to these questions. Make a list of alternative answers. Replace your mother's maiden name with another name, use a different school name, or provide a false birth year. Ask if other questions can be use to verify your account information. This way only you know the question they will ask. And only you will know the answer.

You should make a list of alternative answers to these standard verification questions. If you change your mother's maiden name be sure you remember what you used or you may be denied access to your own information.

Pick up your mail and newspapers daily. If you will be on vacation, stop your mail and newspaper delivery until you return. A pile of papers in the driveway is a sure sign to a thief that you are not at home. Mail piled in a mailbox is an open invitation to steal your statements and bank infor-mation. If you have someone picking up your mail while you are gone, make sure it is someone you would trust with your financial future.

Mail with information labels on the outside of the envelopes can be a real boon to potential thieves. If they know your personal information is inside, they'll definitely want that piece of correspondence. Examples of this include pre-approved offers that state on the envelope "Financial Documents" or "Important Financial Data." Even your insurance envelope may state "Policy and Premium Notice".

Sample "Red Flags" to mail thieves

The first one is stamped "Important Financial Data" the next one "Policy and/or Premium Notice." The next sample shows "tax information." A huge red flag, since it contains more of your personal information than other statements.

Watch your mail closely. Know the dates you usually receive your bank statements, credit card statements, utility bills, and your mortgage statements. If they don't arrive when they usually do, or when you think they should, check to be sure they were mailed on time. Someone could have diverted your mail!

Carefully review ALL your monthly statements and bills. This includes any printed information you receive that could reveal personal information. Look for unauthorized use. Immediately research any purchases, transactions or calls you did not make.

If you are comfortable with online access, cancel your paper bills and statements that come in the mail, if possible, and, instead, check your statements and pay bills online. Monitor your account balances and activity electronically at least once per week.

If you do not have access to online accounts, make sure you review your paper bank and credit card statements monthly and monitor your billing cycles for missing bills or statements.

Use email based account "alerts" to monitor transfers, payments, low balances, and withdrawals. Be sure to review your credit report (now available for free annual review).

Take your payments and outgoing mail directly to the post office. Sending them with the local mail carrier may be convenient, but putting up the flag on your mail box notifies not only your postal carrier, but also thieves that your information is ready to steal. Typically, what's in your mail box includes your bank account information, your signature, and any information on the account you're paying—a veritable smorgasbord for an identity thief. Drop boxes have also been raided by these criminals. In fact, thieves have been known to steal an entire freestanding mailbox. The safest way to mail something is directly through the post office.

Watch your trash. Dumpster divers can obtain mounds of information, especially if it's not shredded. Don't take out your personal trash before it's time for collection because this gives thieves more time to sift through it. Wait until the day of collection.

Secure your personal information at home. We like to think that our home is our castle, our refuge, and our property is safe there. Not so. Do you have children going in and out of your house? repair or service people? cleaning services or maids? a lot of guests? If your information is out in the open, you could easily become a victim. Don't leave your checks, financial statements, bills, or other information lying out on a desk. Put your information in a locked drawer if possible. This includes all your checks, deposit slips, statements, and bills—anything a thief could use to access an account or open a new one.

Make copies of all your credit cards, debit cards, health cards, etc. Copy the front and back of all your cards. If any are stolen, you will have the information available to call and report it. Keep these copies in a safe place, like a locked drawer or safe.

Don't carry every credit card you have and an entire book of checks with you everyday. Checks usually come in a book of twenty to fifty checks. Only carry one credit card and only the checks that you may need for the day. This limits your risk if your wallet or purse is stolen. And you'll know exactly what check numbers are missing. Banks usually don't hold you responsible for the amount of a forged check. But you must contact the bank in a timely manner if your checks are lost or stolen. When a check is taken from the middle or back of your book, you may not realize it is missing until you get that far back in the book. Why take that risk?

Check your health care card. Some PPO's, HMO's, or other insurance cards use your Social Security number as your identification number. If your card does use your SSN and it is printed on the card, make a copy of it. Then, *on the copy*, white out all but the last four numbers of the SSN. Leave the original card in a secure place at home, and carry the copy with the partially obliterated SSN. Once at your healthcare provider's office, you can supply the missing numbers.

If you fill out a loan or credit application or account information form at a business, ask how they will store and/ or dispose of your information. Will it be in an unlocked file that is accessible by all employees? Will they continue to store your information when it is no longer needed? Will they throw away the information or will they shred it?

Find out how many employees will have access to the information. Then make sure it will be stored in locked files or shredded. If you are not certain how your information will be handled or who will have access to it, take your business elsewhere. Some businesses have been known to carelessly handle applications and other personal information, leaving these easily accessible to all employees or other personnel that may have access to that business.

Make it a routine to get copies of your credit reports. Review them carefully. If you don't know how to read a report, ask your banker, CPA, or financial planner to explain it to you. Check for any unauthorized accounts, unauthorized usage, accounts that should have been closed and /or removed. Make sure you check for any "inquiries." Inquires will show up for companies that have accessed your report information in response to a credit request. If you didn't authorize the credit request, it could be an attempt by a thief to open a fraudulent account. Ask that these be removed from your report.

Some states have passed a law prohibiting merchants from recording your SSN or credit card number when you write a check. The merchant may look and these but may not record the numbers or information on your check or anywhere else.

Social Security Numbers,
Who can request them?

Your Social Security number (SSN), the key to your credit and banking accounts, is the prime target of criminals. *PROTECT YOUR SOCIAL SECURITY NUMBER*. Give out it only when absolutely necessary (i.e.., on tax forms, employment records, most banking, stock, and property transactions).

If a business requests your Social Security number, ask if it has an alternative number that can be used instead. Or if it is not an agency that can request your SSN, why substitute another nine digit number? You'll have to remember it as if it was your real SSN.

If the business has a problem with your "fake" SSN ask to speak to a manager or supervisor. Ask to see the company's written policy on Social Security numbers. If necessary, why they are requesting it and how they will secure your information. If they are not willing to accommodate your request, you may want to take your business elsewhere.

Who Can Request Your Social Security Number?

1. Government and Welfare agencies, IRS, State/Local revenue agencies.

2. State Motor Vehicle Departments. If your state uses your SSN as your driver's license number, ask to substitute another number.

3. State professional/occupational/ recreational licensing agencies. Ex.: hunting or fishing licenses, building licenses or permits.

4. Banks, Securities companies, and Brokerages.

5. Employers can ask for your SSN. Don't write your SSN on your application and submit it. You should give it to the prospective employer during your interview or after you are hired.

6. Other government agencies must tell you why they need your SSN. If the SSN is requested by a government agency, look for the Privacy Act notice. This will tell you whether your SSN is required, what will be done with it, and what happens if you refuse to provide it.

7. For an explanation of the meaning of the numbers in your SSN, see "Structure of Social Security Numbers," by Computer Professionals for Social Responsibility, available at *cpsr.org/oldsite/ externalSiteView/cpsr/privacy/ssn/ ssn.structure.html*

Passwords and PINs

When creating passwords, do not use your first or middle name, pet's name, or anything else that might be discovered by thieves. Create passwords that combine letters and numbers.

Personal identification numbers (PINs) must be numbers and are usually 4 to 8 digits. Do not use the last four digits of your Social Security number, your birth date, or any consecutive numbers.

Use passwords on all your accounts. Don't give your password to anyone via email. If you receive an unexpected phone call asking for your password, don't give it out. Find out the name of the person calling you and why they are requesting your password. Politely get off the phone with them and call the company back to verify the person works there and why they need to know your password. Use the company phone number that is printed on your statements. Do not ever use a phone number that the caller gives you. It could be a partner in crime.

Ask your financial institutions to add extra security protection to your account. Most will allow you to add an additional code or password (a number or word) or security questions when accessing your account by phone. Ask that the institution not discuss any of your account information over the phone or in person unless they first are provided with that additional code or password by the person making the request. Do not use items identity thieves can easily obtain such as your mother's maiden name, your SSN, date of birth, etc.

Memorize all your passwords. Don't record them on anything in your wallet or purse. Don't write your password on your ATM card or credit card

Shield your hand when using a bank ATM machine, store PIN Pad, or making long distance phone calls with your phone card. "Shoulder surfers" may be nearby with binoculars or video camera. Block the view with your body or your hand.

Credit Cards

Cancel unused credit cards. It's not enough to just cut up the cards you no longer use. Call and cancel the account. This will help keep your open and legitimate accounts easier to review and verify.

Check your credit card receipts. Merchants should no longer be printing your entire number on the receipt, only the last four or five digits. If the merchant copy has printed your entire number on the receipt, cross out all but the last four digits. You have the right to do this, and once the transaction is captured electronically, your entire number is no longer needed by the merchant. This prevents a thief from gaining access to your credit card information and your signature.

Don't ever leave any receipts anywhere. Don't drive away from the gas pump without checking for your receipt. Don't leave receipts at a restaurant. Don't throw the receipts down or in a trash can placed outside for public use. This gives thieves easy access to your information.

Check your receipts against your monthly statements. Research any unknown charges. If they are not legitimate, report them as soon as possible. Be ready to explain why you know this is not your charge, and stay calm when you're discussing it.

Once again, only carry the cards you will need. If you are going out for one day, only take one card. If you will be on vacation only take the card you will need for expenses. The more cards you carry, the greater your risk if you become a victim of a pickpocket or purse snatcher. If you flash a wallet full of credit cards—even unintentionally—you could become the target of a watchful pickpocket team. They could distract your attention, and you won't even know your wallet is gone until you reach for it later. By then, the crooks are long gone.

In order to take advantage of the $50 limit for unauthorized credit card charges by the Fair Credit Billing Act (FCBA) you must:

1. Write to " Billing Inquires" not Payments.
2. Send your letter within 60 days of the first bill that contains the error.
3. Send your letter certified mail and request a return receipt.
4. Then, the creditor must resolve the dispute within two billing cycles after receiving your letter.

What Does Not Belong on Your Résumé?

Keep in mind that your résumé is not what will get you a job. The purpose of a résumé is to provide a potential employer with enough information to open the door to an interview. During the interview process you may disclose additional information—if you feel comfortable doing so. When writing a résumé, you need to remember that the information you provide could be a gold mine for a potential identity thief. Here are some recommendations for items you should not include in your resume.

The purpose here is not to give a potential thief a source from which he/she can collect additional information. Note in particular that listing schools is optional, and remember that it may be possible to collect information from an alumni source or alumni contacts.

Recommended Items to Eliminate from Your Résumé

- Your SSN should never be written on your résumé
- Your Date of Birth (DOB)
- Marital Status
- Age (It's against the law to ask for this)
- Sex (It's against the law to ask for this)
- Do not list your professional license number
- Disabilities. Unless the job specifies a request up front.
- Hobbies
- EIN (tax identification number if you use an alternate to your SSN
- Driver's license number
- Year you graduated or received a degree from various schools
- School names are a personal choice. If possible designate by football group, such as an Ivy League.
- DO list all your areas of study, any degrees received and areas of special training.

Businesses

Employers should train all employees who have access to personal information on procedures of responsible handling of all private data. They need to adopt privacy policies and make sure all personnel are thoroughly versed in the appropriate uses of personal information. All employees should also know the risks of mishandling information.

Customer information should always be kept confidential. Files should never be left out on a desk, even for a short time. Customer information that can be viewed on a computer screen should also be protected from the view of other employees and customers or vendors who may be in the area. The customer's computer file should never be left open if the employee who has accessed it leaves the area. If the screen can easily be seen by someone near the desk, a privacy block such as a room divider or hanging plant should be considered to obscure the view.

Confidential paperwork and files should always be kept in a secure place when they are not needed. This could be a locked drawer in a desk or, if the volume is large enough, a separate file room with a locked door. If keys are a concern, a lock with a number pad works well.

Businesses must shred confidential papers that are no longer needed and should have specific procedures for handling these types of documents. The following questions need to be addressed by all reputable businesses:

- What is done with papers containing personal information before they are shredded?
- Are documents kept under a desk, in a box, or in a wastebasket until the end of the week?
- Is the pending shred box secure until its contents are shredded?

Pending shred bins must be secure. Appropriate guidelines should be in place to assure that the pending shred bags are not tossed out with the regular trash or left in an area where the cleaning staff could assume them to be office trash that needs to be carried out. This could be a gold mine for a dumpster diver.

Thieves have obtained confidential information by dumpster diving within hours of the bags being placed in the trash. So even if your confidential material will only be unsecured for a short time, it could potentially get into the hands of a thief.

For recommendations on protecting customer privacy and a checklist of Responsible Information-Handling Practices, businesses can visit this web site: *privacyrights.org/fs/fs12-ih2.htm.*

President Bush signed the Fair and Accurate Credit Transactions Act (FACTA) on December 4, 2004. Many of its provisions are being phased in. This affects businesses.

If you employ only one person, including a nanny, housekeeper, or anyone you are paying Social Security taxes for, you must destroy confidential information before throwing it away.

Merchants must leave off all but the last five digits of a credit card number on electronically printed store receipts, effective nationwide on December 2006. This helps reduce access to the credit card information by anyone having access to the receipts.

Employers must destroy information derived from consumer credit reports before discarding them, effective June 1, 2005.

Failure to comply with FACTA provisions could result in a lawsuit, fines, or being named in a class action lawsuit. Federal fines can be as high as $2,500 for each violation and State fines as high as $1,000 per violation.

Irresponsible handling of private information could result in unauthorized access to or out right theft of the documents. Businesses could soon share the consequences of mishandled information along with the thieves that steal it or use it.

Who Else Is You?
How to reduce your risk of becoming an identity theft victim.

Your Work Place

Don't leave outgoing mail in your out box on Fridays. Mail left over the weekend is easy picking for a thief. You probably won't even realize it's been stolen until you find out it was not received. This day is known as "Fraud Friday" indicating that thieves are aware of lax policies and easy access to unsecured information.

Secure personal information at work. Don't leave your briefcase, purse, or backpack on the floor in plain sight. A thief can grab the information they want in a matter of seconds. If possible, lock it in a drawer or locker.

Password protect your computer. Even if you are away from your desk for only a few minutes, it is possible for someone to quickly access your computer.

Don't post your passwords on the side of your computer. Don't save your passwords to pre-load on your computer. These may be convenient for your everyday use, but it leaves a door wide open for a thief to hack into your information, or if you step away from your computer.

Ask your employer how they store your personal information. Is it in a locked drawer or is it accessible to any office person? Thieves are not just looking for client information. Any ones information will do.

Request that your employer implement privacy polices for the storage and destruction of confidential staff files as well as customer files. This type of procedure falls under the FACTA provisions, so it's the law now that your employer has to implement procedures to help protect any confidential information.

Parents

Parents, you have the responsibility to watch out for your children. When your baby is born, he/she receives a Social Security number within a few days. That number will be used to identify your child for the rest of his/her life.

You may not think about checking for fraudulent activity in your children's name until you start a savings account or a college fund for them. That's usually the first time anyone runs a check on a child's Social Security number.

Some children learn they are fraud victims when they attempt to get a driver's permit or a license. So, parents, take the time to check on your child's identity as well as your own.

A thief may use a child's information for years before anyone becomes aware of it. Then it comes not only as a shock, but also with considerable negative effects that can complicate the child's future for decades.

In some cases, the school or a coach may request your child's information for verification purposes. If this happens DO NOT give copies to a secretary or office assistant. Make sure you know who will handle your child's information and how it will be secured.

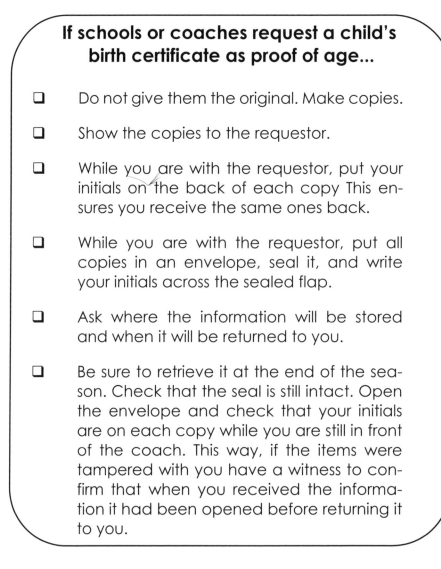

If schools or coaches request a child's birth certificate as proof of age...

❑   Do not give them the original. Make copies.

❑   Show the copies to the requestor.

❑   While you are with the requestor, put your initials on the back of each copy This ensures you receive the same ones back.

❑   While you are with the requestor, put all copies in an envelope, seal it, and write your initials across the sealed flap.

❑   Ask where the information will be stored and when it will be returned to you.

❑   Be sure to retrieve it at the end of the season. Check that the seal is still intact. Open the envelope and check that your initials are on each copy while you are still in front of the coach. This way, if the items were tampered with you have a witness to confirm that when you received the information it had been opened before returning it to you.

If you think someone has taken out student loan in the name of your child you should contact the school or program that opened the student loan. Ask them to close the loan and remove the debt from your child's record. You should also contact the Office of the Inspector General at the Department of Education to report the fraudulent loan. 800-MIS-USED or *ed.gov/offices/OIG/hotline.htm* .

Parents safeguard your child's information

❑ Don't give out your child's information.

❑ Keep the original Birth Certificate and Social Security card in a safe, secure, fireproof place.

❑ If you don't know the person your child will spend time with, such as a coach or day-care provider, do a background check.

Theft
Complaints by Age

Under 18 ...4%
18-29.........29%
30-39..........25%
40-49..........20%
50-59..........12%
60-64...........3%
65 +.............6%

National and State Trends in Fraud & Identity Theft
January – December 2004. FTC Feb. 2005

Students

The largest number of reported victims is between the ages of 19 and 29. Because of their inexperience and lackadaisical financial habits, some students and young people make easy targets for thieves. Here are some tips for young people.

If your school uses your social security number as your student identification number, request that your school use an alternative number for your student identification number.

Don't leave your checkbook, debit card, bank statements, or mail lying out in your room. Keep your information in a secure place, especially if you live in a dorm or have several roommates. People and friends of friends could be in and out of your room, having total access to anything lying on top of a desk or in an unlocked drawer.

Beware of on campus scams. Unscrupulous people may pose as a credit card company or cell phone provider, using applications to get your information.

Don't be intimidated. Take charge of your own protection. Before giving out personal information such as your SSN or other identification, know to whom you're giving it and why they need it. Ask how it will be protected.

Don't store your personal identification information on wireless phones, PDAs, laptops, or other devices. Wireless signals can be used to tap into your devices and upload your information—or to install viruses.

Don't let your credit cards out of your sight. If you pay at a restaurant, try to pay at the register or pay with cash. Don't let someone walk away from your table with your card.

If you live in a dormitory or with roommates, keep your personal information in a safe. Get a small one and keep it locked. Don't leave the key on your desk or in the lock.

Safes come in a variety of sizes and price ranges. A small one will do the trick, and it costs considerably less than having your identity stolen.

Senior citizens

Senior citizens can be especially vulnerable. Even though victims in this category make up the smallest percent of those hit (only nine percent of those sixty years and older), the effects can be devastating. Some have even lost their homes, and the emotional stress can lead to serious medical problems.

The low percentage of victims could be a result of delayed discovery. Many more of you could already be victims, but you just don't know it yet. Many seniors don't need to apply for credit, so there's less opportunity to find errors on your credit reports. Make sure you get a copy of your credit reports and review them closely. If you need to, ask your banker, financial planner or CPA for help understanding the information.

Many of you worked long, hard years to earn good ratings and high credit scores. Often your mortgages are paid off, or you have accumulated large amounts equity. But having worked a lifetime to establish an excellent payment history doesn't help if a thief comes along and ruins that good record. It all goes down the tube. While seniors may have less financial exposure than young people who are just starting out with credit cards, automobiles, and new homes, you do not have a lifetime ahead of you to try to fix the problems.

Thieves may pose as authority figures to intimidate seniors into giving them personal information. They can pose as government agents, law enforcement officers, financial advisors, utility personnel, or some other professional. Their purpose is to convince you that they require your information, and require it right now, for whatever reason they come up with.

It is vital to remember that, when any person tries to gain access to your home or your information, you should verify the company the person represents, verify that the person is actually employed by that company, and verify the reason for requesting your information.

First, don't let the person in your house. Ask what company he/she represents; then ask the person to wait outside while you verify the information. And then close the door. Do NOT allow the person to enter your home. Look up the phone number for the company in the phone book, or call directory assistance. Don't ask the person at your door for the company's number. If you do, you may be given a number for an accomplice, who will, of course, verify the legitimacy of the person at your door. Get the phone number to the company by another means.

Once you reach the company, tell the person to whom you are speaking that you have an employee of that company at your door asking for information. Ask for employment verification of the person at your door. Then ask what information they are requesting. If the company does require information from you, provide it over the phone or offer to send it in written form. Make sure you understand why they need your information.

If the person at your door is impersonating an employee, he or she will likely be gone when you return. And if that's the case, be grateful. You probably have just thwarted someone's attempt to steal your identity or your money. Good for you!

Some senior citizens have learned they are identity theft or fraud victims when they received notification from collection agencies or foreclosure proceedings have been started against them. Unbelievably, some thieves have obtained enough information about their victims to qualify for home equity loans or even to sell the homes right out from under the owners.

Home equity loans are a particularly lucrative method used by thieves, who take out a loan against the equity accumulated in your home. Loan documents are drawn up under the *your* name but the mailing address is changed. You don't know there's a new loan against your home until you are notified by a collection agency.

In some cases the scam involved two thieves. One poses as the property owner (you), the other poses as a buyer. The "owner" sells the property to the buyer, who has obtained financing by using the property (your property) as collateral. The "owner" shows up at the closing and signs over the deed on the property to the buyer and receives the purchase price from the financial institution that is providing financing to the buyer.

The thieves walk away and split the loan proceeds, never intending to pay any of it back. Why should they? The loan is not on their property. Because the loan documents were set up with a false mailing address, none of the payment notices are sent to you, the "real" owner. Eventually, the loan goes into default. The property goes into foreclosure and could eventually be sold on the courthouse steps. As the victim, you are not aware of what is happening with your property until the officials show up to evict you! What a shock. You'll probably have to find another place to live until the whole ordeal is resolved. This is, no doubt, *not* the way you had planned to spend your retirement.

Seniors are also targets for online scams. As people who grew up with simple manual typewriters and strong lessons on the value of honesty and integrity, seniors often do not understand the complexities of the Internet or the magnitude of their exposure to scam artists who hitchhike on the Information Highway.

One common but effective approach by the thieves involves virus protection and pop-up ads. Some of them send out ads that pop up on your monitor and say something like this: "Your computer has just been scanned and several viruses have been detected. Click here for information." When you click the link provided in the pop-up, it takes you to a site that informs you your computer has a particularly dangerous virus, and you need to purchase their virus protection **right now** in order to clean it up and protect you files. Of course, another link is provided for your buying convenience. Many victims are so concerned that they go ahead and purchase the online virus protection.

What's wrong with this picture? First, no one should be able to access your computer from the Internet to run a virus scan. Second, your computer likely doesn't have that particular virus...until you click on their link. Third, they scare you into buying their protection—right now! It's their way of separating you from your money. Not to mention that now they have your credit card information for their future use!

What's the moral here? They're out to get you! Make sure you have current mainstream virus protection such as McAfee® or Norton®. You'll also need spyware protection as well as pop-up protection and a firewall. Then you won't have any reason to fall victim to scams like this one.

Before you spend tons of money on a lot of protection programs, seek the advice of a local computer consultant. Or call the local college for advise.

Computer Users

Some people believe that if they don't access their personal information over the Internet, they will not become victims. But many do not realize that, with all the highly technical systems used by financial institutions today, their information is already floating around in cyberspace, whether they choose to access it or not.

These days, online services are secure and in some ways safer than conventional transactions. With electronic statements and electronic payments, you no longer have to worry about someone stealing your statement or your check out of the mail. If your mail gets diverted to a criminal, you won't have to worry because your statements are all electronic.

> **While only 11% of reported identity theft cases are due to online activity, Internet-related complaints accounted for 53% of these crimes—with losses of over $256 million.**

We should note, however, that online identity theft is often under reported because online theft may be categorized under another felony activity, such as fraud—or the victim fails to inform authorities of the crime.

Obviously, Internet users do need to exercise caution. Know whom you are dealing with and become familiar with the way those online companies do business. Don't assume that a link to a website *always* goes to the "real" site. Think first about what you are doing—and act second. A little thought and inconvenience now may alert you to possible fraudulent sites, emails, and scams, preventing a lot of frustration, potential loss, and huge inconvenience later.

Don't save and pre-load passwords. Don't write your password on a sticky note on the side of your computer. Change your password often, and use a mix of numbers and letters. If your password is case sensitive, mix in upper and lower case letters.

Use a current virus, firewall, and pop up protection program, and keep it updated. Updates come out often since new viruses show up almost every day. Outdated protection is of little use.

Unhide file extensions. This may help reveal unwanted executable programs. For example, with file extensions hidden a file may look like susie/jpg. When you unhide the file extension, it reveals the rest, so it looks like this, susie/jpg.exe, an executable spyware called a Trojan or a worm. Trojans or worms may enter your computer, unbeknown to you, and appear to be dormant, non-threatening programs. Their purpose is to nest and create a spy program to monitor sites you visit. Talk about "big brother" watching!

Do not be intimidated by e-mails threatening to suspend or close your account if you do not immediately verify your information. This is usually an attempt at "phishing" for your information. Never click on the links provided in the email. These often take you to a fake site that mimics the original. It may look exactly like a site you are used to seeing, but it isn't. The link could vary by only one letter. If you believe the contact is legitimate, go to the company's Web site by typing in the site address directly or using a page you have previously book marked. Or telephone the company and ask whether the site you have entered is legitimate and if they really sent the email alert.

Don't open or respond to unknown emails. Many spam blockers help in this area, but we still need to be cautious of unknown emails. Delete them before you open them. If it is a legitimate urgent message, the sender will contact you by traditional means, like snail mail or the telephone.

Don't click on links from unknown email sources. If you receive emails with "Click Here" links or links with which you are unfamiliar, don't go there. If you want to visit the site, type in the web address yourself. Look for website privacy policies. A privacy policy will tell you whether your information will be provided to third parties, how the information will be used, control of information that is collected, and how they will maintain access and security of your information. For more information see "Site-Seeing on the Internet: A Traveler's Guide to Cyberspace" from the FTC at ftc.gov.

Use only secure web browsers and software that encrypts or scrambles the information you send over the Internet. Make sure your browser has up-to-date encryption capabilities by using the latest version available from the manufacturer. Look for the security "lock" icon and secure links indicated by the web site https: prefix (note the "s" following "http," indicating a secure site). Know the sites you visit and whether they use personal information. If they don't—but suddenly do— you may be linked to a fake site.

Delete your personal information prior to disposing of your computer or hard drive. It may take more than deleting files by your keyboard or mouse commands. These files can still be recovered. Use a "wipe" or "format" utility that will overwrite the entire hard drive. More information is available in "Clearing Information from Your Computer's Hard Drive" from the National Aeronautics and Space Administration. You can access this information at hq.nasa.gov/office/oig/hq/harddrive.pdf

Report suspicious e-mails or calls to the Federal Trade Commission through the Internet at *consumer.gov/idtheft* or by calling 1-877-IDTHEFT.

In these fluctuating economic times, everyone seems to be seeking lower mortgage interest rates. We see ads everywhere for low-rate financing, and pop-ups on the Internet are commonplace to the point of annoyance. Be cautious. If the offer sounds too good to be true, it probably is. If you have never heard of the financial institution, call the agencies that have jurisdiction over those institutions and verify that it is a legitimate business.

Becoming Internet-wise and Information Highway-savvy is a must in this day of world-wide community that brings with it a neighborhood larger than anytime in human history. The Web can be a relatively safe place, but learn the strategies that make it that way and keep your portion of it secure.

In early 2005 many people responded to an internet ad for low rate mortgages.

While talking with the representative, prospective clients were told that in order to qualify for the low interest rate, they had to open a bank account with that particular financial institution. A deposit of $4,000.00 was expected.

Clients wanting to take advantage of the low interest rates were willing to send in deposits.

As you guessed it, the bank was not real nor was the mortgage offer. It was all a scam to collect money from innocent people.

Equifax has introduced a tool bar aimed at reducing online identity theft. The tool bar will help consumers measure the safety levels of web sites before you reveal personal information.

Equifax.com

Phishing and Pharming

The word "phishing" was coined to represent scams in which thieves attempt to lure victims into revealing personal information.

Phishing scams have been around since 1996 when hackers started stealing American Online accounts from customers. It has grown very rapidly since that time. The next "phishing" spots are predicted to be wireless and cell phones.

The current hook is an e-mail that appears to be from a legitimate source, such as a bank or financial service. Some of the company names used include CitiBank, PayPal, Bank of America, and TCF Bank, and the list is growing.

> **The number of Phishing sites in 2004 went from 176 in January to 1518 in November, according the Anti-Phishing Work Group. That's a 760% increase in less than a year!**

Phishing scams look very professional and make very real sounding threats. If you receive a request for information from a company you do business with, call the business to verify the request. Don't just assume it to be real. Don't link to web sites from a suspect email, and don't use phone numbers provided in the e-mail. No matter how legitimate it looks – call the telephone number you commonly use before you surrender your information.

Remember: These sites can mimic those of prominent banks, financial institutions, retail stores, and credit card companies. Phishing is increasing by leaps and bounds because it's working. Take precautions! Don't be fooled by a rogue site.

Here are examples of actual e-mail Phishing attempts the author received from two different sources. Their purpose is to gather personal information.

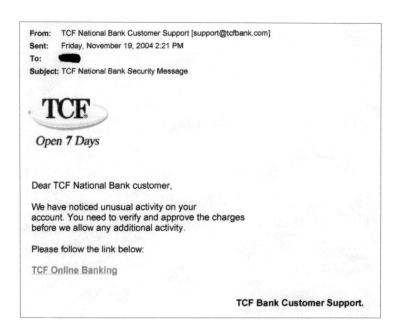

From: TCF National Bank Customer Support [support@tcfbank.com]
Sent: Friday, November 19, 2004 2:21 PM
To:
Subject: TCF National Bank Security Message

TCF
Open 7 Days

Dear TCF National Bank customer,

We have noticed unusual activity on your
account. You need to verify and approve the charges
before we allow any additional activity.

Please follow the link below:

TCF Online Banking

TCF Bank Customer Support.

How were they recognized as fraudulent? First, the author doesn't have accounts with either of these institutions! Second, they contained certain red flags.

As you can see, the one from TCF asks to approve charges and has a link to the online banking site, where it wants account information entered to verify the charges. *Banks don't do business this way!* The e-mail is linked to a fraudulent site that mimics the institution's real site. Right down to the logo, it looks very authentic.

The Charter One e-mail (on the next page) uses a typical ploy: a threat of action. By stating bluntly that the account is in danger of suspension, phishers hope the recipient will feel an urgent need to clear up the issue and maintain access to the account.

Notice that it then says to *wait 48 hours before further action*—after providing the requested information, of course—*so they can investigate the account*. This is "phisher language" for "give me 48 hours before you look to see that all your money is gone."

Note, too, how easy they make it to log in. They conveniently allow the author to use her Social Security number. Again, *the links are not connected to any real bank sites.*

It is imperative to *never* respond to such a situation in an emotional rush. Use your head and reason on the matter. Someone on the other end of that e-mail has probably gone phishing.

From: customerservice@charterone.com

Sent: Monday, February 07, 2005 5:35 PM

To: ▮▮▮▮▮▮▮▮▮▮123.biz

Subject: CHARTERONE NOTICE: possible unauthorized account access

Dear CharterOne customer,

We recently noticed one or more attempts to log in your CharterOne account from a foreign IP address and we have reasons to believe that your account was hijacked by a third party without your authorization.

If you recently accessed your account while traveling, the unusual log in attempts may have initiated by you.

However if you are the rightful holder of the account, click on the link below and submit, as we try to verify your account. (in case you are not enrolled use your Social Security Number as both **User ID** and **Password.**)

https://secure.charterone.com/info/index.aspx

The log in attempt was made from:

IP address: **158.0.55.157**
ISP host: **158-0-55-1.T1fast.net**

If you choose to ignore our request, you leave us no choice but to temporally suspend your account.

We ask that you allow at least 48hrs for the case to be investigated and we strongly recommend not making any changes to your account in that time.

If you received this notice and you are not the authorized account holder, please be aware that

2/11/2005

114

A new threat evolving from Phishing is known as Pharming. This is, potentially, an even more devastating problem. Pharming stems from Phishing but with a twist. Rather than threatening victims into disclosing personal information on fraudulent sites, it enters your computer through a virus, worm, or Trojan. The malware (malicious software) then embeds a program that can take over your tool bar and redirect you from the site you want to go to.

You, as the victim, have no idea you are being sent to a bogus site. You think the website address you typed in will lead you to the legitimate site you want. But despite your typing in the correct site name, you are directed to a fraudulent site somewhere else. There you do business as you would normally. However, the bogus site gets all your information rather than the real one—with potentially devastating consequences for you.

Changes in the DNS (Domain Name Server) protocols and security authorizations may be the only solution to this new threat.

Many companies and politicians are aware of the potential dangers of Pharming and are working on security controls to protect the consumers and stiff penalties for the criminals who take up "Pharming."

Phishing Red Flags

- Threats of disaster, suspending or closing your accounts. These are usually extreme sounding threats.

- Poor grammar and misspelled words. This can happen in legitimate emails, but it is more prevalent in a phishing attempt.

- Unusual characters in the "From" field or message field. Exclamation points or other characters used to complete words or underscore. Like a zero instead of the letter "O", a dollar sign for the letter "S" or the symbol " | " instead of the letter "L".

- Rich content and embedded ads. When a business sends a legitimate email it is usually plain text. Promotional emails may be rich text.

Scams: What to Watch for

Scams are so numerous, because they are so effective. People fall victim to them everyday, and they are often associated with computer or online fraud. But in addition to fraudulent e-mails and web sites, a phone call or someone knocking on the front door can bring a scam right into your home. The best way to fight against becoming the victim of a scam is to *know* with whom you are talking. If you did not originate a call or request a visit from a vacuum cleaner salesman, etc., get some type of verifiable identification from the person you are talking to. Call the company to be sure such a person exists and represents the company *before* giving out any personal information. Then ask to be connected with that employee while you are on the line. If the caller is legitimate, he/she will appreciate your conscientiousness.

Following are a few of the most popular scams.

- E-mail Email tracking schemes. These schemes were originally created to plant spyware or other tracking programs and spread them through e-mails. These usually appear as a "warm and fuzzy" message requesting that you send this happy thought to everyone on your e-mail list. If you choose to do as the message requests and pass it on, re-write and send it alone. Don't hit the forward button and send a mass message.

- You've won a free...whatever. No, you haven't. It's a scam to collect your information. Delete the message. The ploy is that you must pay for shipping and handling. To pay this charge, you must give them your account information. Or they may tell you they want to send you money. Again, they will ask for your account information. Either way, your money will be leaving your account.

- Help move money from my country. This successful scam has found many willing victims who have bought the hard luck story of the thieves. It keeps circulating because it works. People fall for this every day. Think about it...why would someone from another country contact you—a person they do *not* know—and tell you they'll pay you to help them get their own money? It's either money laundering or money obtained by illegal means or, most likely, a scam to steal *your* money!

- Money has been credited to your account. "Click Here to Verify." Or click "yes" or "no" to verify. This may refer to an online pay account such as PayPal or to your bank accounts. If you click to verify, you will probably be linked to the website that belongs to a thief. But if, for some reason, you think it's legitimate, call the company directly and ask.

- Canadian/Netherlands (or other countries) Lottery Winner. Many people buy into this scam. An e-mail announces you've won the lottery, but if you haven't bought a lottery ticket, you *can't* win the lottery! Nonetheless, they claim to need your information in order to wire your winnings directly into your account. What happens? You give them your information. Your money disappears. Next is an example of a winning lottery letter.

C/CORDOBA NO 21 PLANTA 2-A
28204 MADRID ESPAÑA
TEL: + FAX: 00 34 625-802-884

DATE: 25TH SEPTEMBER 2003 .

FROM: THE DESK OF THE VICE PRESIDENT
INTERNATIONAL PROMOTIONS/PRIZE AWARD DEPT
REF NO: EGS/25512/56003/03
BATCH NO: 1490/001753V00/IPD

ATTN: F   R.
RE: AWARD NOTIFICATION, FINAL NOTICE.

We are pleased to inform you of the release today 20TH SEPTEMBER on the results of the **EL GORDO SPANISH SWEEPSTAKE LOTTERY/NEWYEAR HIGHSTAKE INTERNATIONAL PROGRAM** held on 28th of JANUARY 2003.

Your name attached to the ticket number 025 – 11464992 – 750 with serial number 2113 – 05 drew the lucky numbers 13 – 15 – 22 – 37 – 39 – 45 which consequently won the lottery in the 3rd category.

You have therefore been approved for a lump sum payout of <u>US$815,960.00 (EIGHT HUNDRED AND FIFTEEN THOUSAND, NINE HUNDRED AND SIXTY US DOLLARS)</u> in cash credited to file **REF.NO: EGS/2551256003/03**.This from a total cash prize of **US$13,871,320.00 (THIRTEEN MILLION, EIGHT HUNDRED AND SEVENTY ONE THOUSAND, THREE HUNDRED AND TWENTY US DOLLARS)** shared among the international winners in this category.
CONGRATULATIONS! .

Your fund is now deposited with a security company and insured in your name already with insurance bond policy coverage. Due to mixed up of some numbers and names, we ask that you keep this award from public notice until your claim has been processed and your money remitted to your nominated account, as this is a part of our security protocol to avoid double claiming or unwarranted taking advantage of this program by participants. All participants were selected through a computer ballot system drawn from 25,000 names from USA, Canada, Europe,Middel East,Asia and Africa as part of our international program, which we conduct once every year. We hope with a part of your prize money, you will take part in our mid year (summer) high stake US$1.6 billion international lottery.

To begin your claim, please complete the enclosed release order form, and send by fax to your claims agent, **DON PEDRO BANDERAS** Foreign Operations Manager, **ATLANTICO GRUPO SEGURIDAD S.A** ON TEL: 00 34 635-343-776 , FAX: 00 34 635-343-228 for processing and remittance of your prize money to a designated account of your choice. Remember, all prize money must be claimed not later than 30TH OCTOBER 2003. After this date all funds will be returned to the MINISTERIO DE ECONOMIA Y HACIENDA as unclaimed.

NOTE: In order to avoid unnecessary delays and complications, please remember to quote your reference and batch numbers in every of your correspondence with us or our agent Furthermore, should there be any change of your address, do inform your claims agent as soon as possible. Congratulations again from all members of our staff and thank you for being a part of our promotional program.

Sincerely.

DON ANTONIO MYER
(VICE PRESIDENT)

Along with the winning lottery letter, there will be an information form which requires your full name, bank name, bank ABA or routing number, your account number and any other information they think they can get out of you.

The requirement is, you must supply them with your bank information in order to receive your winnings. The only winnings you will ever see is that of becoming one of the "chosen few" who innocently allow total strangers full access to your bank account and your money.

Who Else Is You?
How to reduce your risk of becoming an identity theft victim.

Chapter 10
How Did They Get My Address?

You may have grown up hearing that your mail is private, and certainly postal regulations protect the privacy of certain types of mail. However, your name and address are *not* private. In fact, your mailbox has probably been flooded with sales ads, prize offers, and catalogs—more than once, most likely. The majority of these you probably did not request and may not have wanted.

Did you know that information about where you do business and how you manage your bills is made available to marketing companies through credit bureaus? While they do not share specific information such as how much you owe or to whom, they do use your information to compile lists based on the characteristics of consumers. This means that your information is grouped with others similar to you to compile lists that fit a specific set of criteria.

Let's look at an example. A list could include people with incomes over $40,000 who use credit cards and pay on time. One who falls into this category would receive mail from the purchaser of that list. This could include "pre-approved" credit card offers, catalogs, or any other unwanted mail.

When you make a purchase from one mail order company, it is likely you will receive offers from other companies as well. How does this happen? Many companies "rent" their mailing lists. These include mail order companies, credit card companies, and magazine distributors. Depending on your interests, you may receive catalogs, special offers, or sales ads for related items. If you like gardening and subscribe to an organic gardening magazine, you may also receive offers or catalogs for nutritional supplements and natural foods from companies who want your business.

When you provide your name and address to a business, you could be added to a database somewhere. Making a substantial purchase like a car or buying from a catalog, completing a product registration card, or having a baby may well put you on somebody's "list."

When you purchase goods through a mail order catalog, your name is added to a database that is sold to other mail order companies, who will then send you their catalogs and offers. The Direct Marketing Association (DMA) and Abacus are companies that compile these cooperative databases. The databases are provided to publishing companies and catalog companies for a fee.

Many credit card companies compile lists of cardholders for sales promotions, based on buying habits and patterns. Cardholders, however, have the option to prevent the release of their information. To do this, the cardholder must contact the credit card company by phone or mail and request the appropriate form to remove his/her name from the "list."

The White Pages of the telephone book lists your name, address, and phone number. These are public records. Mailing list companies can collect and sell this information to mail order companies and marketing firms. The phone company and other companies also compile directories organized by address and phone number rather than by name. If you are listed in the White Pages, you are also in one or more of these "street address directories," also known as "reverse directories."

When you purchase a product, your receipt should serve as evidence of the warranty if that product is defective. Usually, you needn't send in the registration card. However, some manufacturers prefer that you register your purchase in case of a product safety recall. If you do decide to send it in, don't include more information than necessary. Your name, address, product serial number, and date of purchase should be adequate.

Major lifestyle changes can end up in the public records when a government agency records the event. What events are so public? Birth certificates, marriage licenses, and home sales are but a few. Companies wanting your business access public records. For example, new parents may begin to receive advertisements for baby items within days after their child is born.

Government records about you usually cannot be kept confidential. If you find you are on a mailing list compiled from public records, you must contact the companies individually if you want to be removed from their list.

When you move and submit a change of address form to the post office, the U.S. Postal Service (USPS) provides your new address to mailers who have your old address. This reduces the amount of misaddressed mail they have to handle. That's one of the ways unsolicited mail is able to follow you around. If you don't submit a change of address form to the USPS, you must contact everyone you from whom you want to receive mail, Including your bank(s), mortgage company, utility companies, your family, and friends. It may be easier to try to stop the unwanted mail rather than miss giving your new address to any important correspondents.

Charities and non-profits often exchange or rent lists from one another. So if you have ever donated to any one of these, chances are you have received solicitations from other related organizations.

When you register in a contest or sweepstakes, you are likely giving information that will be on a list used by another contest, sweepstakes, or lottery company.

The Driver's Privacy Protection Act allows the sharing of personal information with law enforcement officials, courts, government agencies, private investigators, and insurance underwriters, along with some other similar businesses. It does not allow personal information to be distributed to direct marketers.

The lists go on and on, but you can minimize the "junk mail" that seems to keep coming your way. Persistence is the key. You will probably not get rid of all your unwanted correspondence, but keep after it. Likely, you can reduce the amount you do receive.

Chapter 11
How Can I get Off These Mailing Lists?

Getting onto the myriad of lists that result in a barrage of junk mail coming your way is pretty much automatic. No muss. No fuss. No effort. No permission. Getting off those lists is another matter entirely. Muss. Fuss. Effort. Perseverance. But it *can* be done!

The two major companies that sell lists based on county property records are Dataquick (877) 970-9171 and Acxiom (877) 774-2094. Call these companies to opt-out of their public records marketing lists.

Direct Marketing Association (DMA) and Abacus are companies that compile cooperative databases. Contact each of them to request your name be included in their opt-out program. This should notify all the companies that participate with this program.

You must individually contact the companies that do not participate in the Direct Marketing Association and Abacus opt-out program. Call, e-mail, or write to the customer service departments and request that your name and address not be provided to other companies. You must

127

also contact any company that does not participate with DMA or Abacus. This includes magazines, charities, non-profit organizations, and professional organizations to which you have donated or joined and any other company from which you continue to receive unwanted mail.

If you do not want to receive pre-approved credit offers you should call toll free 888-5-OPT-OUT.

Consider having an unlisted telephone number. Or request that the local phone company publish just your name and phone number and omit your address. Ask the phone company to remove your listing from its "street address directory." Call or write the major directory companies, Haines & Company, Inc. and Equifax (formerly Polk), requesting that your listing be removed.

When you send money to a charity or nonprofit group, include a letter requesting the organization not rent, sell, or exchange your name and address. If you receive solicitations from other groups, you may have to do some detective work in order to be deleted from their mailing list. Since these groups rent lists, they cannot delete your name from those that have already gone out. However, the mailings generated by these lists will have a "reply device" and mailing label that likely contain codes indicating the list that included your name. You can ask the organization that mailed you the solicitation where the list came from and the name of the organization that provided it. Then you can contact that organization to remove your name from their list and request your name not be rented, sold, or exchanged.

If you really want to enter a contest, check to see whether they have an "opt out" option so you can avoid having your name added to a mailing list. Read through the small print and beware of scams. Is the prize too good to be true? Do you have to pay a fee up front to get the prize or gift? If so, it's probably a scam. In April 2000 a federal law became effective that allows consumers to more easily be removed from sweepstakes mailing lists. The Deceptive Mail Prevention and Enforcement Act requires the mailer to provide its name and address on the solicitation, including an address or toll-free number to request removal from the company's mailing list. Fraudulent companies often ignore this law, and many lottery mailers and sweepstakes are from other countries that are not covered under this law.

When you send in a warranty or product registration card, you are probably joining a mailing list. Often these cards ask for information that is not required by the company to guarantee the product. These often query you about your hobbies, your income, the number of people in your household, number of TV sets, etc. Furthermore, these registration cards are generally not mailed to the company that manufactured the product. Typically, they are addressed to a company that compiles buyer profiles, then sells these lists to other businesses for marketing purposes. The registration card usually goes to a post office box in Denver, Colorado, for Equifax (which was formerly Polk), or to Experian.

You also have an avenue to reduce the number of commercial e-mails you get. Contact the Direct Marketing Association through its website. This won't stop all unwanted e-mails, nor will it stop spam. But it will help limit commercial e-mails that you receive.

If you buy a house and begin receiving home improvement or insurance solicitations you do not want, contact the companies. Ask to be removed from their mailing lists. The name of the company distributing the mail should be printed on the piece of mail somewhere. Generally it is printed in the paid postage area.

Look at the postage area on the next piece of unsolicited mail you receive. You may see the name of the distributing company who has your name on a list, and the sender may be the same as the distributing company. If so, the address should be in the upper left corner. If not, look in the other printed areas for an address.

Compare your mail to the sample shown here. Can you find the distribution company's name and address?

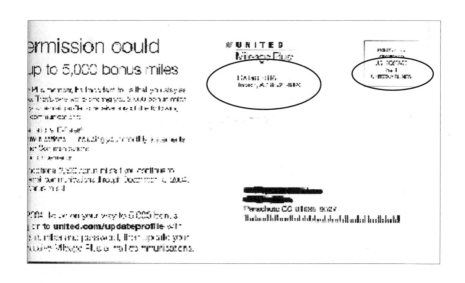

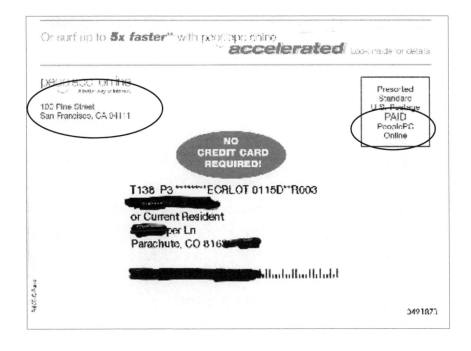

Or surf up to **5x faster** with peoplepc online
accelerated Look inside for details

peoplepc online
A better way of life.

100 Pine Street
San Francisco, CA 94111

Presorted
Standard
U.S. Postage
PAID
PeoplePC
Online

NO
CREDIT CARD
REQUIRED!

T138 P3 *******ECRLOT 0115D**R003

or Current Resident
per Ln
Parachute, CO 816

0491871

To have your name removed from the major nationwide sweepstakes mailers, contact the following companies. None of these rents their lists.

Publishers Clearinghouse
101 Channel Dr,
Port Washington NY 11050
800-645-9242

Readers Digest Sweepstakes
Readers Digest Road
Pleasantville NY 10570

American Family Publishers
PO Box 62000
Tampa FL 33662

One way to reduce junk mail is to write to Equifax and Experian to be removed from their survey mailing lists.

Equifax
 Direct Marketing Solutions
Consumer Response Center
26955 Northwestern Hwy, Suite 200,
Southfield, MI 48034-8455
(800) 873-7655

Experian
Consumer Services
901 W. Bond St.
Lincoln, NE 68521.
(800) 407-1088.

Who Else Is You?
How to reduce your risk of becoming an identity theft victim.

National Lists

To remove your name and address from most national mailing lists, contact the mailing list company Abacus and the Direct Marketing Association's (DMA) Mail Preference Service (MPS). With DMA, you must re-register after five years, but it also has a resource for you if you are trying to help your elderly relatives remove their names from sweepstakes or other types of contests.

You may want to receive some unsolicited mail, such as catalogs or special offers. If this is the case, don't contact the Direct Marketing Association's Mail Preference Service. You will have to notify all companies individually if you don't want their unsolicited mail. You will also need to ask the companies you do want marketing materials from to keep your name and address private. Otherwise, they could rent or sell it to another marketing company. Look for this "opt-out" option in their literature.

Every company should have a disclosure notice and "opt-out" option. It's good business for them to offer privacy safeguards, so if you don't see a notice, ask the company.

Mailing Lists

1) Direct Marketing Association's
   Mail Preference Service (MPS)

   Mail Preference Service
   PO Box 643, Carmel NY 10512
   the-dma.org/consumers/offmailinglist.html

   Telephone Preference Service
   PO Box 1559, Carmel NY 10512
   the-dma.org/consumers/offtelephonelist.html

   Internet access
   dmaconsumers.org/ consumerassistance.html
   dmaconsumers.org/privacy.html/privacy.html

   Sweepstakes Helpline,
   1111 19th Street NW, Suite 1100,
   Washington, D.C. 20036 -3603.
   Telephone: (202) 861-2475. Fax: (202) 955-0085
   E-mail: sweepstakes@the-dma.org

   E-mail Preference Service
   dmaconsumers.org/offemaillist.html

2)   Abacus
     To opt-out of the Abacus database, write to
     Abacus, PO Box 1478, Broomfield, CO 80038
     Email: optout@abacus-direct.com
     Include your full name and current address (plus
     previous address if you have recently moved).

3)   Privacy Rights Center (PRC)
     privacyrights.org/Letters/letters.htm#Junk_Mail.
     Here you can access a form letter that is sent to
     subscribing organizations several times a year.
     You are put into a "delete" file. Within three to
     four months you should see a reduced number of
     unwanted mail.

4)   Envelopes with "Address Correction Requested"
     or "Return Postage Guaranteed" can be re-
     turned UNOPENED by writing "Refused - Return to
     Sender" on the envelope. The company pays the
     return postage.

5)   Dataquick
     To opt-out of Dataquick's lists compiled from
     county public record
      call toll-free: (877) 970-9171.

6)   Acxiom
     To opt-out of lists compiled from county public
     records, contact Acxiom's Consumer Advocate
     Hotline at (877) 774-2094
     E-mail *optout@acxiom.com*

Phone Lists

Do Not Call Registry
888-382-1222
Donotcall.gov
For State Registries;
ftc.gov/bcp/conline/edcams/donotcall/statelist.html

Haines & Company, Inc.,
Criss-Cross Directory
Attn: Director of Data Processing,
8050 Freedom Ave. N.W.,
North Canton, OH 44720.
Send a letter requesting that your listing be removed.
Participates in the Mail Preference Service.

Equifax (formerly Polk),
Attn: List Suppression File,
26955 Northwestern Hwy.
SouthField, MI 48034.
(800) 873-7655.
Give your name, address, and phone number.

More on Junk Mail

Your local Postal Inspector takes complaints about mail fraud, theft, tampering, and obscene or pornographic mail. Use U.S. Post Office Form 1500 to notify the Post Office of any sexually explicit mailers or marketers sending you unwanted mail. If you use this form, the offending companies should stop mailing to you. To obtain a copy of this form, visit your Post Office or go online to usps.gov.

❑ ☐ Junkbusters – sample letters and tips
Junkbusters.com/junkmail.html

❑ ☐ Privacy Rights Center
Privacyrights.org/Letters/letters.html#Junk_Mail

❑ ☐ Consumer Research Institute
Stopjunk.com/environment.html

❑ ☐ Obviously Implementations Corp
Obviously.com/junkmail

❑ ☐ Ecofuture
Ecofuture.org/junkmail.html

❑ ☐ Good Advice Press
offers a pamphlet: "Stop Junk Mail Forever"
$4.50 (includes postage and handling)
P.O. Box 78, Elizaville, NY 12523
800-255-0899
goodadvicepress.com

❑ ☐ Private Citizen
offers a junk mail reduction service (for a fee)
Box 233, Naperville, IL 60566
800-CUT-JUNK
Private-citizen.com

Who Else Is You?
How to reduce your risk of becoming an identity theft victim.

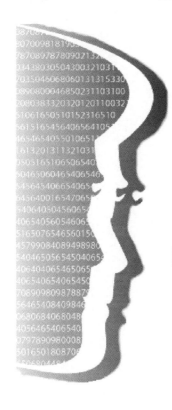

Section Three: Get Organized

Before You Become A Victim
If You Become A Victim
Recovery: How Long?
Basic Steps For a Victim
Specific Problems
Credit Bureaus
Services
Laws

Who Else Is You?
How to reduce your risk of becoming an identity theft victim.

Chapter 12
Before You Become A Victim

Get organized...*before* you become a victim!

Begin by monitoring your statements each month. In the Plan of Action section, you will find a worksheet to help you accomplish this. First, you need to know the approximate time you receive your statements each month. Watch for them to arrive. If one fails to show up when it is due, this could be a sign that something is wrong. Statements that don't arrive on time may have been diverted to a different address, or a thief could have stolen them from your mailbox.

Review your statements for any unauthorized activity. Don't just glance at the balance—*look at the transactions*. Compare your activity with the activity listed on the statements. Are they all yours? Are the amounts correct?

Watch for very small charges. Some unscrupulous companies have added additional charges that they hope consumers will not notice it, or will not take the time to dispute. Some companies combine several billing companies on one statement. They do not know what is a legitimate charge and what isn't. They just compile the charges they receive from these other companies.

An example of a company that combines several billings on one statement could be your phone bill. You usually receive one statement that has several carrier services charged through that single statement. A $2.00 charge could easily slip by you, and thousands of other people. Making a quick profit for crooked companies.

Also monitor your credit reports. Order current copies from all three major credit bureaus. You can obtain one free report per year from each bureau. You will find information on the three major credit bureaus in the Resources section.

To better monitor activity, don't order all three reports at the same time. Order one report now or at the first of the year. Then wait four months and order the second one. Wait an additional four months to order the third one. This way you can check a different report every four months and watch for suspicious activity or inquiries.

The cycle of ordering your three reports should last one year. You will start the new year by ordering from the first bureau again, then the second, and the third, each time waiting four months before ordering the next one. A worksheet is provided in the forms section to assist you with organizing your credit bureau monitoring efforts.

Chapter 13
If You Become A Victim

If you do become a victim, you already know the ride will be long and difficult. To make the process as smooth as a bumpy ride can be, start with an organized course of action.

The things you do now will either help you or hinder you later, so keep good records. In fact, keep everything. Make notes about all that happens and everybody you talk to, including dates and details of each conversation. Get the name and phone number of everyone you deal with. In the Plan of Action section, charts are provided to help keep you organized during this process.

Write down the accounts involved and the specifics of how you learned about the fraud. Keep all the documentation or information that brought it to your attention.

Keep the originals of all supporting documentation, including but not limited to police reports and letters from creditors. If you need to provide documentation to law enforcement or an involved business, *don't send the origi-nals*. Put all original documents in a secure place and make a copy to keep with your files.

Through the course of recovery, creditors or other businesses involved may require a police report as proof of a crime. File that now—while the information is fresh. Make it a priority, but be prepared for an uphill battle. Police officers may or may not be helpful, especially in larger cities where they are overburdened with what they may consider to be *real* crimes. You are a victim here. Insist on your right to file an appropriate report. Also, be sure you get the help you need to complete that report correctly. Make it as detailed as you can. Don't skimp on any information. If local law enforcement does not provide adequate sup-port, consider county or state law enforcement officers.

If you use a recovery service, confirm whether you should file the police report or whether the company pro-viding the recovery assistance will do it. Don't assume they will file a report for you, but if they tell you they will, follow up yourself to make sure it has been done. Regardless of who files the report, do it as soon as possible and insist on having a copy of it for your records.

On accounts opened by an identity thief in your name, you will not have any paperwork to show that you didn't do it. In this case, you can use an "ID Theft Affidavit." The Federal Trade Commission (FTC) designed this form in conjunction with banks, creditors, and consumer advo-cates. Available at *ftc.gov/idtheft*. The purpose is to help you close unauthorized accounts and eliminate fraudulent debts associated with you. Not all companies will accept this form, however. They may have one of their own. Ask each company involved to see what its policy is in ID theft cases.

Keep all the correspondence you receive. Keep copies of your credit reports, police reports, and copies of the disputed bills or fraud issues.

Write down the names of everyone you talk to. Keep notes on everything he/she told you and the dates of the conversation. Use the worksheets included in this book to help organize your information. Follow up in writing with every contact you have made by phone or in person. In this letter, give an account of the conversation you had with that person. Include as much detail as possible and copies, (not originals) of any supporting documentation they require. Make a copy of your letter for your file.

Because this letter may provide the only evidence of your contact with that person, send it certified mail, return receipt requested. Then you have proof that they received your written follow up and/or any other information you may need to send.

One of the largest complaints by victims has been the lack of responsiveness from the companies involved. Many victims have had to repeatedly send supporting documentation, and yet company personnel denied ever receiving their information—even when the victims provided the return receipt signed by a company employee. So be forewarned that you may encounter this reaction from some companies.

Because of the attitude of many companies, along with the hours it steals from your life, more and more people are opting for recovery assistance services. When an attorney or professional gets involved companies seem to be more likely to cooperate with your recovery.

Some services will only guide you along your way, others will take the reigns until it's resolved. For more information on one such company go to: *prepaidlegal.com/idt/csgraham*.

If you decide to pursue recovery yourself, be persistent and be firm, but don't lose your temper when you deal with them. Getting angry will only hinder your case because no one will want to deal with you. Nor will anyone want to help you resolve your issues. In fact, they may not be willing to work on your case, at all. Even going so far as not returning your phone calls or your correspondence.

So be patient. But be persistent.

Chapter 14
Recovery, How Long Does it Take?

The recovery process is a long and arduous journey. It takes a lot of time to compile the information needed, to make phone calls, write correspondence, and whatever else you must do to clear your name. Victims spend an average of 600 hours in the course of their recovery.

Clearing your name is only part of the process. Inaccurate information can reappear even after you think everything has returned to normal. And the cycle will start all over again.

Some victims of criminal identity theft have had to travel to a different state just to prove to law enforcement officials that they do not match the description of the wanted criminal. While most victims will not face that sort of burden, the time involved in clearing your name can be overwhelming.

The recovery process often involves taking time off work. As if that weren't enough, victims may spend their vacation days trying to clear their names rather than enjoying recreation or time spent with family. They also use sick days. But these paid days off are sometimes inadequate to get the job done.

As a result, some have had to take time off without pay to resolve the problems they have encountered since becoming a victim of identity theft. This boils down to less time, less money, and more stress for those victims who are just trying to get their lives back.

Lost wages because of missed workdays can be devastating, and for many will add to the already high levels of stress. Even for those on salary, 600 hours spent trying the resolve the issue of identity theft equates to losing fifteen weeks of work. That's almost four months! Most people cannot afford to miss that much work. But unless you have arranged for an alternate source of recovery assistance, you will have to buy out the time somewhere to meet those 600 average hours. Most companies you will be contacting are only available during regular working hours. This could mean the time you buy out will have to come from your job.

Because of tougher confidentiality policies, you may find it difficult to get the documentation you need from a creditor or financial institution to prove you did not make the transaction in question. Even though this seems like the law is protecting the criminal at the expense of the victim, you must remain calm. Remember that all employees must adhere to their company's disclosure polices.

If you complete the creditor's fraud paperwork or an ID Theft Affidavit, most of the time, you—the victim—can get the accounts closed and the debts dismissed. However, you will need to submit a copy of your police report along with the ID Theft Affidavit or other fraud paperwork.

Once you are satisfied that the matter is cleared up, insist on a letter from the institution stating that the account in dispute has been closed and any fraudulent charges against you have been dismissed. If errors come up later, or the negative information about you is re-circulated, you will be glad you have this information on hand. It will be powerful evidence in your behalf as you work to convince debt collectors, credit bureaus, and authorities that you are the innocent victim of someone else's crime. It may even help to resolve the problems that will pop up down the road.

Now you know that the process will the lengthy. Be prepared. Get organized!

Victims spent an average of 600 hours in their recovery.

According to a report by the FTC
"Identity Theft: The Aftermath" published in 2003.

Who Else Is You?
How to reduce your risk of becoming an identity theft victim.

Chapter 15
Basic Steps for a Victim

These are the basic steps to take as soon as you believe or suspect you are a victim. Additional information about contacts can be found in the Resources section of this book.

1)   File a report with the Federal Trade Commission (FTC) Identity Theft Hotline. The FTC maintains a database of identity theft cases and assists victims of these crimes by providing information. While the FTC does not have the authority to give legal advice or bring criminal cases, your input helps to provide knowledge that may assist law enforcement agencies in tracking down and stopping identity thieves. This is particularly important because you may not be the only victim in your area. FTC counselors will take your complaint and give you advice on how to deal with the problems that could result. They are available at 1-877-IDTHEFT (438-4338).

2.   If you have an identity protection plan provided by a legal service, call them as soon as possible. They will usually collect information from you and, if you so desire, take over the recovery process for you. This is a great benefit to anyone who doesn't have the time to chase down information, make lengthy phone calls, or visit agencies.

3.   You should complete an ID Theft Affidavit. The FTC, in conjunction with banks, credit offices, and consumer advocates, created this form. A form is available online at the ID Theft Website: *consumer.gov/idtheft*. Some businesses may not accept this form, or they may have their own. But filling one out is a good place to start as you implement your course of action.

4.   Make a police report, keeping several copies for yourself. Furnish as much information as you can to prove your case, including all debt collection letters, credit reports, a notarized ID Theft Affidavit, and any other information to support evidence of fraudulent activity. You may need to be persistent because local authorities may tell you they can't take a report. This could create a "catch 22" situation because many creditors *require* a copy of a police report to resolve your dispute. So be the "squeaky wheel that gets the grease" if your law enforcement agency drags its feet in accepting your report.

5.   Ask the police department to search the FTC's Consumer Sentinel database for other complaints in your community. You may not be the first in your community to report a problem. If there is other fraudulent activity in your area, local authorities may take your case seriously.

6. Call the credit bureaus. Tell them you believe you are a victim of identity theft or fraud. Follow up in writing, including copies of your credit report with the fraudulent items circled. Also include copies—not originals—of your police report, ID Theft Affidavit, and any paperwork you received from the creditor or documentation of calls you received from the creditor or collection agencies.

7 Request that fraud alerts and victim's statement be placed on your credit files with all three major credit bureaus. A victim's statement asks creditors to call you personally before opening any new accounts or changing existing accounts. This helps prevent an identity thief from opening new accounts in your name.

8. Call the creditor, financial institution, or other information provider. They usually have a fraud department. Follow up in writing. Provide copies—not originals—of the same documentation provided to the credit bureaus.

9. Close all accounts that you believe have been opened fraudulently or have unauthorized usage.

10. Notify your bank or financial institution that you are a victim of fraud associated with other accounts. Ask that they place a higher level of security access on your account, perhaps implementing passwords or verification questions. And limit the access to your account.

11. If you think an identity thief is using your SSN, call the Social Security Fraud Hotline at 1-800-269-0271. If you think someone may be using your SSN to work, check your Social Security Personal Earnings and Benefit Statement. You can get a copy by calling 1-800-772-1213, or online at *ssa.gov/online/ssa-7004.pdf*. Also see the Social Security Administration's booklet "When Someone Misuses Your Number," available at *ssa.gov/pubs/10064.html*.

---

11 Basic Steps For A Victim

1. File a report with the FTC Identification Hotline.

2. Contact your legal service plan provider or attorney.

3. Complete an ID Theft Affidavit.

4. Make a police report.

5. Search the FTC's Consumer Sentinel Database.

6. Call the credit bureaus.

7. Place Fraud Alerts and Victim's statements on your credit reports.

8. Call the creditor(s).

9. Close the account(s).

10. Notify your bank.

11. Call the Social Security Fraud Hotline.

Chapter 16
Do You Have Specific Problems?

Specific problems require specific actions.

Again, it takes a lot of time to clear up unauthorized use of your name or credit—situations where the thief impersonated you (cloning) or engaged in criminal activity, using your identification. All these areas can impact your life for years to come. Resolving the problems quickly, on the other hand, will help reduce the number of incidents that could occur. The sooner you know about the situation, the easier it will be to resolve.

Here are some specific problems with suggestions about what to do to help resolve them. If you suspect you have become a victim of any type of identity theft or fraud, take action right away. If you have an Identity Theft plan through a legal provider, contact that provider immediately. If you don't have an Identity Theft plan, you can call the FTC's Identity Theft Hotline toll free at 877-IDTHEFT (438-4338) or go online to *consumer.gov/idtheft* for guidance.

Debt Collectors Keep Calling Me!

If you are being hounded by calls from debt collectors about fraudulent accounts or charges, you need to know about the Fair Debt Collections Practices Act. Under this act collectors are prohibited from using unfair or deceptive practices to collect overdue bills that a creditor has forwarded for collection.

To stop the calls from a debt collector, write a letter to the collection agency, telling them to stop. Send it registered, return receipt requested. This way you can verify the agency received it. Once the debt collector has your letter in hand, the company cannot contact you again—with the exception of two calls: One to tell you they will not contact you again and the other to tell you that they intend to take some specific action.

If you send the collection agency a letter stating you do not owe the money within thirty days after you receive written notice from them, they cannot contact you. Include copies of any supporting documents you have along with your letter. This way a collector should not be able to renew the collection activities based on some other proof of debt.

Even though you will gain some peace of mind when the calls and notices stop, you need to realize the debt itself has not been eliminated. *That* can still show up on your credit report.

If you send documentation establishing that you did not authorize the accounts or debt, it becomes the debt collectors' responsibility to prove that you did. Your documentation should include a copy of the fraudulent application for credit, which you should have already obtained.

This application will contain the thief's signature and alternate address. You can prove that the signature is not yours by providing evidence of your own signature on a copy of your driver's license, passport, etc. You should check with the agency to learn what type of evidence they prefer.

As a side note, if a debt collector insists on a small or partial payment in order to stop the collection calls, you should be aware that you could be re-affirming the debt if you make a payment. If you have concerns or suspect it is an old debt of your own, seek the advice of your attorney or credit counselor before you pay.

These Aren't My Credit Card Charges

If you have unauthorized charges on your credit card, the Truth in Lending Act limits your liability for those charges to $50 per card. However, you must follow the procedures established by the Fair Credit Billing Act to resolve these errors.

First, you must send a letter to the credit card company, stating your name, address, account number, and description of the unauthorized charge, including the amount and date of the charge.

Do not mail it to the same address where you send your credit card payments. You must send it to the address given for "BILLING INQUIRIES." You may want to call the credit card company to ensure that you send the information to the correct address.

The creditor must receive your letter within 60 days of the date the bill containing the unauthorized charge was mailed to you. In the event that the thief changed your mailing address and you did not receive the statement, the creditor must resolve the dispute within two billing cycles, but not more than 90 days, from the receipt of your letter. A sample letter is included in the forms section.

These Debits Aren't Mine

Unlike credit card debt, the amount you can be held liable for on an ATM card, debit card, or electronic fund transfer depends on how quickly you report the loss. The Electronic Fund Transfer Act provides protection from unauthorized transactions and limits your liability for unauthorized use if you report it in a timely manner,

Visa and MasterCard voluntarily limit consumers' liability for unauthorized use , in most cases, to $50. With the increase in losses the expense has to be passed along somewhere. We all may end up paying more for service fees or products to help cover their losses.

If you discover unauthorized transactions, contact the financial institution and follow up the call with a letter stating the same information you gave over the phone. Send the letter certified mail, return receipt requested. This way you can prove the institution received written confirmation of your call. After receiving your notification of an error, the institution generally has ten days to investigate the problem. They must tell you the results within three business days of concluding their investigation. If they find an error, they have one business day in which to correct it.

In some cases more time may be required to thoroughly research the problem. If this is the case, they can take up to 45 days— but only if you are given provisional credit. This means the funds in question are returned to your account, and you are sent a notice of the credit. If, after their investigation, they determine that no error has occurred, they should send you a written notice of their findings. The money can then be withdrawn from your account.

My Bank Won't Help Me

If you are having trouble getting help from your bank or financial institution, other avenues of assistance are open to you. Financial institutions operate under the jurisdiction of regulating agencies. A list of these agencies is included in the Resource section of this book. If you don't know which one to contact, call the institution and ask. You can also access information on line at *ffiec.gov/enforcment.htm.*

If your ATM card is lost or stolen and you report it within two businesses days, your losses are limited to $50

If you do not discover the unauthorized use right away but report it within 60 days of the statement showing the unauthorized use, you can be liable for up to $500.

If you wait more than 60 days you could be liable for ALL the money taken from your account.

Electronic Funds Transfer Act

What Happened to My Investment Accounts

If a thief wants access your investment accounts, he/she can get to them as easily as your bank accounts. Review your statements each month, and make sure you understand how to read them. Your banker or financial planner will be glad to review your statements with you. Keep an eye on activity, watching for unauthorized access to your account.

If you suspect an identity thief has tampered with your accounts, report it immediately to your broker or account manager. You can contact the U.S. Securities and Exchange Commission (SEC) if you suspect fraudulent activity from your broker or firm. The SEC has an online Complaint Center at *sec/gov/complaint.shtml.*

Someone Filed Bankruptcy in My Name

Some identity thieves have filed for bankruptcy under another person's name and Social Security number. Why would an imposter want to do this, especially since you're the one collection agencies will come after? Some do it to avoid being evicted or want to keep on "being you" and avoid the debts they have incurred.

If this happens to you, write to the U.S. Trustee in the area where the bankruptcy was filed. You can find a list of the U.S. Trustee Program's Regional Offices available on the U.S. Trustee website, usdoj.gov/ust, or check the Blue Pages of your phone book under U. S. Government Bankruptcy Administration.

In your letter describe the situation and provide proof of your identity. They may make a criminal referral to law enforcement authorities if you provide appropriate documentation to substantiate your claim.

The U.S. Trustee will not provide legal assistance or representation. You may have to hire an attorney to convince the bankruptcy court that the filing is fraudulent and to obtain copies of court documents. For a fee you can also obtain copies of court documents from the bankruptcy clerk's office. You can file a complaint with the District Attorney in the city where the bankruptcy was filed. It might be wise to file a complaint with the FBI in that same area.

I'm Wanted By the Police

Imposters using your name and identification can make false reports that result in arrest warrants, traffic citations, or criminal convictions in your name. Efforts to clear your name can be difficult as well as time consuming. If you have an identity theft plan or a legal service plan, contact the service for help. If you don't have a legal plan, you may need to use your one phone call from jail to contact a criminal defense attorney to assist you.

When trying to correct your record in the criminal justice databases, you may find that procedures vary from county to county and state to state. Generally, you can contact the court that ordered the warrant for the person using your identity or the arresting or citing law enforcement agency where the original arrest of your imposter took place.

File an impersonation report and have your identity confirmed. To do this go to the police department and have them take a full set of fingerprints along with your photograph. Also supply them with copies of any photo identification you have, such as our driver's license, passport, or visa. Ask the department to compare your fingerprints against those of the imposter. If the crime took place in another state, ask your local police department to send your impersonation report to the police in the jurisdiction where the crime originated. This is time consuming for the police, but you need to prove you are the not the criminal they are looking for.

If you have been arrested, and you have proven that you are not the criminal they are looking for, ask for a recall of any warrants and request a "clearance letter" or certificate of release. This letter may come from the state's bureau of investigations. Make sure you carry a copy of this letter with you at all times, keeping the original in a safe, secure, and, if possible, fire proof place. You will need this anytime law enforcement decides to look for the name they have associated with the crime.

The follow-up investigation should establish your innocence. Ask the law enforcement agency to file a record of the that investigation with the district attorney's office or court where the crime took place.

It is likely that once your name is in the criminal database, it will never be removed. However, you may ask the law enforcement agency to remove your name as the "key" or "primary" name on the criminal file and change it to the imposter's name or to "John Doe" if the imposter's name is not yet known. Request that your name be listed only as an alias.

Your name will also be on the records of the court where the prosecution took place. Find out which state law will help you remove your name form the those records. If you live in a state that does not have a formal procedure for clearing your name, contact the district attorney's office where the case was originally prosecuted. You will need copies of the appropriate court records in order to clear your name.

During all this, you should contact the department of motor vehicles in the state where the prosecution took place and in your own state to learn whether an imposter is using your driver's license.

My Passport is Lost or Stolen

If your passport has been lost or stolen, you should notify the passport office of the State Department in writing. Let them know the details of how or where you believe your passport was lost or stolen. They should be on the watch for anyone ordering a new passport in your name. You can get information at travel.state.gov/passport_services.html or find a local field office listed in the Blue pages or your telephone directory

I Think Someone Has Diverted My Mail

If you suspect that someone has stolen your mail or has diverted it with a false change-of-address request, you should contact your local postal inspector. Give the inspector all the details, including the reason(s) you suspect your mail has been diverted or stolen. To find the name of your local postal inspector, call your post office. You can also access this information online at *usps.gov/website/depart/ inspect.*

I Think Someone's Using My SSN

If you suspect that someone else is using your Social Security number to obtain employment or credit, contact the Social Security Administration's fraud hotline 800-269-0271. You should order a copy of your Personal Earnings and Benefits Estimate Statement and review it for any errors. You can also request a copy of this statement at your local Social Security office, or you can download one from *ssa.gov/online/ssa-7004.pdf*

Someone is Using My Driver's License Number

Imposters using your name and identification may attempt to get a driver's license or state identification card. If you suspect someone is using your name, contact your state's Department of Motor Vehicles (DMV). If you live in a state that uses your Social Security number on your driver's license number, ask to have another number substituted in its place.

You can check with the DMV for any misinformation reported against your license. You may, however, have to pay a fee of one to ten dollars for the report. Review the report carefully, notifying the DMV of any erroneous information.

It could be that you are not aware of anything until you try to renew your own driver's license. You may be denied due to unpaid tickets, reported fines, criminal activity, unpaid child support, outstanding warrants or a host of other offenses committed by your imposter. Until things are cleared up you may not be able to renew your license. This is another instance where you may want the advice of an attorney or your legal service provider.

My Child Has Lost Personal Documents

If child has lost originals or copies of personal documents, such as a birth certificate, passport, or Social Security card, don't assume that nothing will happen because your child is young and has no credit history. A thief can use copies of personal information to gain access to additional data, perhaps even altering certain portions of the original documents to make them a "better fit."

Consider, for instance, a birth certificate. A thief can use it to acquire a state identification card or driver's license. Or a thief can obtain your child's SSN and clone his/her identity to use in committing criminal acts.

Thieves can go undetected for many years by simply using a child's information rather than an adult's. Current statistics indicate identity theft and fraud for youngsters is low, but this could increase when young victims themselves apply for a driver's license or state identification and learn that their names have been assumed by some unscrupulous person(s).

Parents should check their child's credit history and Social Security report. Also, keep checking with the Department of Motor Vehicles for any records that may appear on a driver's license issued under your child's information.

Chapter 17
Credit Bureaus

When you report suspected fraud, the credit bureaus have thirty days to complete an investigation, forty-five days if you provide additional documentation. If the credit bureau believes you did not provide enough documentation to support your claim, or they consider the claim frivolous, they must notify you within five business days. All documentation you furnish is sent to the information provider—the company that issues the credit or other information—for them to research.

After the investigation, the credit bureau must give you the results in writing. If any changes were made to your credit report, they must provide you with a free copy of it.

If the credit bureau decides to change the information, the bureaus cannot put any item back that was changed or removed unless the information provider verifies it to be accurate and complete. They must then give you written notice regarding the information. That notice should include the name, address, and phone number of the information provider.

If you ask—and you have to ask—the credit bureau must send out a notice of correction to anyone who received your report in the last six months. If a credit report was issued due to a job application, a notice of correction can be sent to anyone who received a copy in the last two years.

If your issue is not resolved through the investigation, ask the credit bureau to include a 100-word statement of the dispute for your file and to include that dispute statement with future reports.

The bad news is, the credit bureau may charge you for fixing your own report. Make sure you state that you are a *victim of identity theft*. This may help to waive any fees charged to you.

Here are some examples of information that should be corrected or deleted from your credit file

- Inaccurate information. The information provider must notify any credit bureaus it reports to so the credit bureaus can correct your file.

- Disputed items that cannot be verified must be deleted from your file.

- Errors. Any erroneous information must be corrected by the credit bureaus.

- Incomplete information must be completed. For example, if you have been delinquent in your payments but the payments are now current, the credit bureau must be informed that you are now current.

Contact the Three Major
Credit Bureau Reporting Agencies.

Equifax
To order your report: 800-685-1111
To report fraud: 800-525-6258
TDD 800-255-0056
PO Box 740241, Atlanta GA 30374-0241
Equifax.com

Experian
To order your report:
 888-EXPERIAN (397-3742)
To report fraud: 888-EXPERIAN (397-3742)
TDD 800-972-0322
PO Box 9532, Allen TX 75013
Experian.com

TransUnion
To order your report: 800-888-4213
To report fraud: 800-680-7289
TDD 877-553-7803
 Fax 714-447-6034
Email fvad@transunion.com
PO Box 6790, Fullerton CA 92834-6790
Transunion.com

Who Else Is You?
How to reduce your risk of becoming an identity theft victim.

Chapter 18
Helpful Services

There are several types of services to help you with monitoring and recovery. However, you need to decide how much *you* want to be involved in the monitoring process, recovery costs, and recovery time.

Do you want to figure everything out on your own?

Do you want to have guidance and phone assistance, while you do all the work?

Or do you want to explain the situation and let a professional take over and do it for you?

How much are you willing to spend for services?

These are questions you should ask yourself before you become a victim so you can have the protection you want when you need it.

Out-of-pocket expenses may become an issue for you when you become a victim. Money could be tight due to lack of funds, access to funds, or credit denials as a result of the thief's activities.

Check with your insurance agent. Some homeowners' insurance policies may cover at least part of the out-of pocket-expenses. Additional insurance polices can be obtained specifically for expenses related to your recovery process. You must weigh the information, cost and then decide what is best for you.

If you want a service that will provide early detection on a continuous basis, look for one that will help you now— *before* you become a victim. Early detection services watch for warning signs, watch your credit report, and, ideally, will provide early detection.

The Identity Theft Shield™ offers an early detection service that looks for red flags that indicate early signs of a problem. It also assists with your recovery process. If you so desire, their trained professionals will do everything for you, or they can guide you through the process. They monitor your credit reports before you become a victim. However, you need to subscribe to this service prior to becoming a victim in order to take advantage of their services. This service at $9.95 - $12.95 per month is well worth the price.

If you know you are already a victim of identity theft or fraud, you can contact a company that will provide recovery assistance to you. Identity THEFT 911 is such a company. It will help with the recovery process and will monitor your credit reports and accounts for a year to provide detection of new problems and to confirm that any fraudulent entries are cleared up. If you want assistance and you suspect your are already a victim, this is a good service.

Remember, whether you use a service or not, you should always call the Identity Theft Hotline provided by the Federal Trade Commission.

Identity Theft Shield™

The Identity Theft Shield gives you easy access to the resources you need to understand your credit ratings and to fight back if an identity thief threatens your financial standings. For information, call your local Independent Associate, Steve Graham, at 970-285-1581 or email at csgraham@prepaidlegal.com or online at *prepaidlegal.com/idt/csgraham*

Identity Theft 911™

This company offers an identity theft solution. They help victims with one-on-one, start-to-finish guidance by a trained, dedicated expert— a personal advocate who understands every aspect of this crime and ensures that each detail gets the attention it needs to accomplish a positive recovery. Users of Identity Theft 911™ crisis resolution services pay a one-time fee. The rate varies according to the classification of your case, determined during an initial interview.
877-ID-CRIME or *identitytheft911.com*
Takeover of existing accounts: $300,
Identity fraud and complex cases: $500.

Legal Service Plans

Legal service plans are becoming more and more popular. Many employers are including legal service plans with their benefits packages.

Legal service plans work much the same way a health care plan or dental plan does. The most common basic legal services are provided with your monthly fee. Additional services are available at a reduced cost.

The attorneys who work with the law firms that provide legal service plans are good attorneys.

Similar to your health care coverage, just because some procedures are covered or are provided at a reduced rate, doesn't mean the health care providers are less qualified.

With a legal plan you have an attorney available to discuss your situation or concerns. Many times just having the advice of an attorney will give you the guidance that you need.

There are several companies that offer legal service plans. Find one that fits your needs. For more information on a great legal plan or identity theft plan go to *prepaidlegal.com/hub/rhoadesw* or contact Jim Rhoades at rhoadesw@prepaidlegal.com

Chapter 19
Aren't There Any Laws Against This?

Identity theft is a federal crime. The Identity Theft and Assumption Deterrence Act was enacted by Congress in October 1998. Under this Act, a name or SSN is considered a "means of identification along with a credit card number, cellular telephone electronic serial number, or any other piece of information that may be used alone or in conjunction with other information to identity a specific individual."

Most states have passed laws related to identity theft, but your state may not have a specific identity theft law. However, the illegal activities of an identity thief are no doubt covered under different statutes, and you may need to seek justice by examining the crimes in which the thief was involved that are addressed by the laws of your state. In this case, an attorney would be helpful. Ask your legal plan provider or contact your State Attorney General's office or consumer protection agency for information.

Identity theft often includes elements of other crimes or fraudulent activities such as:

· Check and credit card fraud
· Forgery and counterfeiting
· Theft and burglary
· Embezzlement
· Cyber-crime

Identity theft can be linked to:

· Mail theft
· Domestic abuse
· Child ID theft/exploitation
· Elderly abuse/exploitation
· Home and vehicular break-ins
· Computer breaches/hacking
· Street gangs and organized pickpocket gangs
· Illegal immigration and human trafficking
· Homeland security
· Narcotics and other compulsive behaviors

Is Identity Theft a Crime in My State?

Alabama-Alabama Code § 13A-8-190 through 201
    (search Alabama Code for "Identity Theft")
Alaska-Alaska Stat § 11.46.565
Arizona-Ariz. Rev. Stat. § 13-2008
Arkansas-Ark. Code Ann. § 5-37-227
California-Cal. Penal Code § 530.5-8
Colorado-Does not have specific ID Theft law.
Connecticut-Conn. Stat. § 53a-129a
    (criminal) Conn. Stat. § 52-571h (civil)
Delaware-Del. Code Ann. tit. II, § 854
District of Columbia-Does not have specific ID Theft law.
Florida-Fla. Stat. Ann. § 817.568
Georgia-Ga. Code Ann. § 16-9-120, through 128
Hawaii-HI Rev. Stat. § 708-839.6-8
Idaho-Idaho Code § 18-3126 (criminal)
Illinois-720 Ill. Comp. Stat. 5/16 G
Indiana-Ind. Code § 35-43-5-3.5
Iowa-Iowa Code § 715A.8 (criminal)
Iowa Code § 714.16.B (civil)
Kansas-Kan. Stat. Ann. § 21-4018
Kentucky-Ky. Rev. Stat. Ann. § 514.160
Louisiana-La. Rev. Stat. Ann. § 14:67.16
Maine-ME Rev. Stat. Ann. tit. 17-A § 905-A
Maryland-Md. Code Ann. art. 27 § 231
Massachusetts-Mass. Gen. Laws ch. 266, § 37E
Michigan-Mich. Comp. Laws § 750.285
Minnesota-Minn. Stat. Ann. § 609.527
Mississippi-Miss. Code Ann. § 97-19-85
Missouri-Mo. Rev. Stat. § 570.223
Montana-Mon. Code Ann. § 45-6-332
Nebraska-NE Rev. Stat. § 28-608 & 620
Nevada-Nev. Rev. State. § 205.463-465
New Hampshire-N.H. Rev. Stat. Ann. § 638:26
New Jersey-N.J. Stat. Ann. § 2C:21-17
New Mexico-N.M. Stat. Ann. § 30-16-24.1

New York-NY CLS Penal § 190.77-190.84
North Carolina-N.C. Gen. Stat. § 14-113.20-23
North Dakota-N.D.C.C. § 12.1-23-11
    (See consumer protection)
Ohio-Ohio Rev. Code Ann. § 2913.49
Oklahoma-Okla. Stat. tit. 21, § 1533.1
Oregon-Or. Rev. Stat. § 165.800
Pennsylvania-18 Pa. Cons. State § 4120
Rhode Island-R.I. Gen. Laws § 11-49.1-1
South Carolina-S.C. Code Ann. § 16-13-500, 501
South Dakota-S.D. Codified Laws § 22-30A-3.1.
Tennessee-TCA § 39-14-150 (criminal) TCA § 47-18-2101 (civil)
Texas-Tex. Penal Code § 32.51
Utah-Utah Code Ann. § 76-6-1101-1104
Vermont-Does not have specific ID Theft law.
Virginia-Va. Code Ann. § 18.2-186.3
Washington-Wash. Rev. Code § 9.35.020
West Virginia-W. Va. Code § 61-3-54
Wisconsin-Wis. Stat. § 943.201
Wyoming-Wyo. Stat. Ann. § 6-3-901

U.S. Territories-
Guam-9 Guam Code Ann. § 46.80
U.S. Virgin Islands-Does not have specific ID Theft law.

Section Four : Resources

Direct mail
Medical Information Bureau
Federal Trade Commission
Check verification companies
Online Resources
Services
Agencies with jurisdiction
Alphabetical Listing of all resources

Direct Marketing

Direct Marketing Association (DMA)
Mail Preference Service (MPS)
P.O. Box 643
Carmel, NY 10512
dmaconsumers.org/cgi/offmailinglist
Opt out by mail is free but could take 30 days
Opt out online is $5 but is faster.

Direct Marketing Association
Telephone Preference Service (TPS)
PO Box 1559
Carmel, NY 10512
Opt out by mail is free but could take 30 days
Opt out online is $5 but is faster.
dmaconsumers.org/cgi/offtelephone

Direct Marketing Association
E-Mail Preference Service (EPS)
dmaconsumers.org/consumers/optoutform_emps.shtml
There is no charge to opt out of EPS

Abacus Alliances
111 Eighth Avenue ,10th Floor
New York, NY 10011
212-683-0001
212-287-1203
optout@abacus-direct.com

Publishers Clearinghouse
101 Channel Dr.
Port Washington, NY 11050.
800-645-9242

Readers Digest Sweepstakes
Readers Digest Rd.
Pleasantville NY 10570

American Family Publishers
P.O. Box 62000
Tampa FL 33662.

Helpful Agencies

Medical Information Bureau
MIB Inc.
P.O. Box 105
Essex Station, Boston MA 02112
617-426-3660
mib.com

Federal Trade Commission (FTC)
877-IDTHEFT (438-4338)
consumer.gov/idtheft

Identity Theft Clearinghouse
Federal Trade Commission
600 Pennsylvania Avenue, NW
Washington, DC 20580

Equifax Toolbar
for combating online pop-ups and intruders.
equifax.com

Check verification companies

CheckRite 800-766-2748

ChexSystems 800-428-9623   (closed checking accounts)

CrossCheck 800-522-1900

Equifax 800-437-5120

TeleCheck 800-710-9898 or 927-0188

Certegy, Inc. 800-437-5120

International Check Services 800-631-9656

SCAN   800-262-7771

Assistance Services

Call For Action (Assistance)
866-ID-HOTLINE

US Department of State
Passport Services
Consular Lost/Stolen Passport Section
1111 19th Street N.W. Suite 500
Washington, DC 20046
Phone 202-955-0430
travel.state.gov/report_ppt.html

United States Postal Service
To find the address and telephone number of
your local postal inspector, go to
usps.com/ncsc/locators/find-is.html
Stolen or fraudulent change of address issues go to
Usps.goc/website/depart/inspect

Social Security Administration
Fraud Hotline
PO Box 17768
Baltimore, MD 21235
800-269-0271 • TTY 866-501-2101
ssa.gov/online/ssa-7004.pdf
Request a copy of your Social Security Statement or verify
 earnings reported call 800-772-1213 or
 ssa.gov/mystatement
To get a replacement SSN card call 800-772-1213
oig.hotline@ssa.gov
Ssa.gov/pubs/idtheft.htm

Identity Theft 911™
877-ID-CRIME
identitytheft 911.com

Identity Theft Shield™
For more information contact
CS Graham, Independent Associate
csgraham@prepaidlegal.com
prepaidlegal.com/idt/csgraham
970-285-1581

Agencies with Jurisdiction over Financial Institutions

Federal Deposit Insurance Corporation (FDIC)
The FDIC secures deposits at banks and savings and loans. It also supervises state chartered banks that are not members of the Federal Reserve System.

Federal Deposit Insurance Corporation
Division of Compliance and Consumer Affairs
550 17th Street, NW
Washington, DC 20429
Consumer Call Center 800-934-3342
fdic.gov

Federal Reserve System (Fed)
The Fed supervises state chartered banks that are members of the Federal Reserve System.
Contact the Fed in your area; there are 12 reserves located in Boston, New York, Philadelphia, Cleveland, Richmond, Atlanta, Chicago, St. Louis, Minneapolis, Kansas City, Dallas, and San Francisco.

Division of Consumer and Community Affairs
Mail Stop 801
Federal Reserve Board
Washington, DC 20551
202-452-3693.
Federalreserve.gov

National   Credit   Union   Administration   (NCUA)

The NCUA charters, supervises, and insures deposits at federal credit unions and many state credit unions.

Compliance Officer
National Credit Union Administration,
1775 Duke Street
Alexandria, VA 22314
703-518-6460
Nuca.gov

Office of the Comptroller of the Currency (OCC)

The OCC charters and supervises national banks. If the word "National" appears in the name of the bank or the letters "N.A." follows the name, the OCC oversees its operations.

1301 McKinney Street
Suite 3710
Houston, TX 77010
800-613-6743
occ.treas.gov

Office of Thrift Supervision (OTS)

The OTS regulates all federal and many state chartered thrift institutions. This includes savings banks as well as savings and loans.

1700 G Street, NW,
Washington, DC 20552
202-906-6000
ots.treas.gov

U.S. Securities and Exchange Commission. (SEC)

The SEC services investors who complain about investment fraud or mishandling of investments.

SEC Office of Investor Education and Assistance
 450 Fifth Street, NW,
Washington DC 20549
 202-942-7040
sec.gov/complaint.shtml

Alphabetical listing of resources

Abacus Alliances (Direct Marketing)
   111 Eighth Avenue ,10th Floor
   New York, NY 10011
   212-683-000; 212-287-1203; optout@abacus-direct.com

Acxiom (877) 774-2094

American Family Publishers (Sweepstakes)
   P.O. Box 62000, Tampa FL 33662.

Call For Action (Assistance)
   866-ID-HOTLINE

Certegy, Inc. 800-437-5120 (Check verification)

CheckRite 800-766-2748 (Check verification)

ChexSystems 800-428-9623   (Check verification closed
      checking accounts)

Consumer Research Institute
      Stopjunk.com/environment.html

CrossCheck 800-522-1900 (Check verification)

Dataquick (877) 970-9171

Direct Marketing Association (DMA)
   Mail Preference Service P.O. Box 643 Carmel, NY 10512
      dmaconsumers.org/cgi/offmailinglist
   Telephone Preference Service (TPS), PO Box 1559,
      Carmel, NY 10512
      dmaconsumers.org/cgi/offtelephone
   E-Mail Preference Service (EPS)
      dmaconsumers.org/consumers/
   optoutform_emps.shtml
   Internet access, dmaconsumers.org/
   consumerassistance.html dmaconsumers.org/
   privacy.html/privacy.html

Direct Marketing Association (Continued)
Sweepstakes Help line, 1111 19th Street NW, Suite 1100,
Washington, D.C. 20036-3603; (202) 861-2475; Fax: (202)
955-0085; sweepstakes@the-dma.org

Do Not Call Registry, 888-382-1222: *Donotcall.gov*
For State Registries:
ftc.gov/bcp/conline/edcams/donotcall/statelist.html

Ecofuture, *Ecofuture.org/junkmail.html*

Equifax (formerly Polk),
Attn: List Suppression File, 26955 Northwestern Hwy.
SouthField, MI 48034 ; (800) 873-7655.

Equifax 800-437-5120 , Toolbar *equifax.com*

Equifax : Direct Marketing Solutions, Consumer Response
Center, 26955 Northwestern Hwy, Suite 200,Southfield, MI
48034-8455 ; (800) 873-7655

Equifax, Credit Report: 800-685-1111; Report fraud: 800-525-
6258; TDD 800-255-0056
PO Box 740241, Atlanta GA 30374-0241; *Equifax.com*

Experian; Credit Report: 888-EXPERIAN (397-3742)
Report fraud: 888-EXPERIAN (397-3742)
TDD 800-972-0322
PO Box 9532, Allen TX 75013; *Experian.com*

Federal Deposit Insurance Corporation (FDIC)
Division of Compliance and Consumer Affairs
550 17th Street, NW, Washington, DC 20429
Consumer Call Center 800-934-3342; *fdic.gov*

Federal Reserve System (Fed)
Division of Consumer and Community Affairs
Mail Stop 801, Federal Reserve Board, Washington, DC
20551
202-452-3693; *Federalreserve.gov*

Federal Trade Commission (Assistance)
  Identity Theft Clearinghouse
  600 Pennsylvania Avenue, NW
  Washington, DC 20580
  877-IDTHEFT (438-4338) ; *consumer.gov/idtheft*

Good Advice Press, P.O. Box 78, Elizaville, NY 12523
    800-255-0899; *goodadvicepress.com*

Haines & Company, Inc., Criss-Cross Directory
  Attn: Director of Data Processing,
  8050 Freedom Ave. N.W., North Canton, OH 44720.

International Check Services 800-631-9656 (
  Check verification)

Identity Theft 911™ (Assistance)
  877-ID-CRIME; *identitytheft 911.com*

Identity Theft Shield™ (Assistance)
  For more information contact
  CS Graham, Independent Associate
  csgraham@prepaidlegal.com
  prepaidlegal.com/idt/csgraham
  970-285-1581

Junkbusters, *Junkbusters.com/junkmail.html*

Medical Information Bureau, MIB Inc.
  P.O. Box 105, Essex Station, Boston MA 02112
  617-426-3660; *mib.com*

National Credit Union Administration (NCUA)
  Compliance Officer,
  National Credit Union Administration,
  1775 Duke Street, Alexandria, VA 22314
  703-518-6460; *Nuca.gov*

Obviously Implementations Corp, *Obviously.com/junkmail*

Office of the Comptroller of the Currency (OCC)
    1301 McKinney Street, Suite 3710, Houston, TX 77010
    800-613-6743; *occ.treas.gov*

Office of Thrift Supervision (OTS)
    1700 G Street, NW, Washington, DC 20552
    202-906-6000; *ots.treas.gov*

Privacy Rights Center
    Privacyrights.org/Letters/letters.html#Junk_Mail

Private Citizen, Box 233, Naperville, IL 60566; 800-CUT-JUNK
    Private-citizen.com

Publishers Clearinghouse
    101 Channel Dr., Port Washington, NY 11050.
    800-645-9242

Readers Digest Sweepstakes,
    Readers Digest Rd, Pleasantville, NY 10570.

SCAN   800-262-7771 (Check verification)

Social Security Administration
    Fraud Hotline, PO Box 17768, Baltimore, MD 21235
    800-269-0271 • TTY 866-501-2101
    ssa.gov/online/ssa-7004.pdf
    Social Security Statement or verify earnings 800-772-1213
    ssa.gov/mystatement
    Replacement SSN card 800-772-1213
    oig.hotline@ssa.gov
    Ssa.gov/pubs/idtheft.htm

TeleCheck 800-710-9898 or 927-0188 (Check verification)

TransUnion, Credit Report: 800-888-4213
    Report fraud: 800-680-7289
    TDD 877-553-7803, Fax 714-447-6034
    Email fvad@transunion.com
    PO Box 6790, Fullerton CA 92834-6790, *Transunion.com*

US Department of State
    Consular Lost/Stolen Passport Section
    1111 19th Street N.W. Suite 500, Washington, DC 20046
    Phone 202-955-0430; *travel.state..gov/report_ppt.html*

US Postal Service, Local postal inspector
    usps.com/ncsc/locators/find-is.html
    Stolen or fraudulent change of address issues go to
    Usps.goc/website/depart/inspect

US Securities and Exchange Commission. (SEC)
    SEC Office of Investor Education and Assistance
    450 Fifth Street, NW, Washington DC 20549
    202-942-7040; *sec.gov/complaint.shtml*

Who Else Is You?
How to reduce your risk of becoming an identity theft victim.

Section Five:
Action Plan Worksheets

Why Worksheets?
How to Use Them

Who Else Is You?
How to reduce your risk of becoming an identity theft victim.

Chapters 20
Why Worksheets?

Worksheets are included as a guide to help you organize your current information and to begin the process of recovery if you become a victim. Feel free to write on these pages so your information and resources will be easily accessible to you *and* in one location. Then put this book in a *secure* place, as it will contain all your personal account data.

It is a good idea to keep one clean original for future use. Make additional copies of the enclosed forms, if necessary.

If you have the capability and the desire to do so, you can use a computer program to remind yourself when it is time for tasks. Use the charts as a guide to enter task reminders into your program calendar. Make sure you save it as recurring so it will signal you at the same time each month.

For example, if you receive your bank statement on the first of every month, you can schedule a reminder that will pop up a day or two before you expect it to arrive. The reminder can say "bank statement" or anything else to bring to mind that you need to watch the mail for it. If you don't have a computer or don't possess the "know-how" or program to set up automatic reminders, you can mark your wall or desk calendar in a similar fashion. Whatever system you choose—and it certainly isn't essential that it be a computer—the key is *consistency*. In other words, USE IT!

Early detection is of paramount importance in limiting the damage caused by a thief and implementing an effective recovery process. Needless to say, it could significantly diminish the stress involved as well.

Here is a list of the charts included:

Monthly Statement Monitoring Chart
Annual Monitoring Activity Chart
Suspect Account List
Financial Institutions Alert Form
Victim Activity Chart (four pages)
Sample Letters

Chapter 21
How To Use The Worksheets

Monthly Statement Monitoring Chart

This chart is designed to help you monitor when you receive your monthly statements. It has listings for checking and savings accounts, investment accounts, mortgage, home equity loan, cell phone, insurance, and credit cards.

The statement type is listed on the left. The next column identifies the account, possibly the account number or a nickname. A nickname could be "my account" or "Steve's credit card" or "house account." Whatever you call it, you must be able to distinguish it from other similar accounts.

The months are listed at the top of the chart. When you receive a statement, write down the date you receive it under the corresponding month. (See example on next page.) Do this for each statement type. If you have additional statements you want to track, add them in the blank lines.

This purpose of this chart is to begin your monitoring process by letting you to know when to expect your statements to arrive. If you notice a statement that should have arrives about the 10th of the month still hasn't arrived by the 18th , it means you should do some digging to find out why. You may have to take steps to prevent a potential problem.

Example Monitoring Form

Acct Type	Acct Name	Due / Arrived	Due / Arrived	Due / Arrived
		Jan	Feb	Mar
Checking	Mine	12th /	12th /	12th /
Checking	Hubby's	16th /	16th /	16th /
Savings	Kids	2nd /	2nd /	2nd /
Savings	Joint	20th /	20th /	20th /
Mortgage	House	15th /	15th /	15th /
Cell Phone	Mine	26th /	26th /	26th /
Credit Card	Hubby's	28th /	28th /	28th /

Annual Monitoring Activity Chart

The Annual Monitoring Activity Chart is designed to organize your annual monitoring tasks. It lists the three major credit bureaus, as well as the Social Security Administration, Medical Information Bureau, and the Local Department of Motor Vehicles. Contact each of these agencies annually to check your reports.

Suspect Account List

This list helps you, first, to chart the type(s) of account(s) on which you suspect unauthorized activity, whether these are checking or savings accounts, credit card, cell phone or utility account, or whatever is in question.

Next, write down the financial institution with that account. This would be the *bank name* in the case of a checking or savings account and/or the *name* of the issuing credit card company (not Visa or MasterCard). Include the telephone number of the financial institution. This will make it easy to access when you need to call them, and your documentation will be at your fingertips.

Be sure to record the date(s) of the suspicious activity and all information you can about the transaction in the comments section.

Financial Institutions Alert Form

Use this form to contact the financial institutions in-volved. Let them know that you suspect you are a victim of identity theft or fraud. Discuss the details of the unauthor-ized transaction with them.

If your checks have been stolen or misused, call the check verification company and tell them which checks were stolen and why you suspect fraudulent activity on your account.

When contacting anyone by phone, make sure you write down the name of the person you talk to as well as the date. Make notes of your conversation. Follow up your phone call with a letter and write down the date you send it. Make sure you keep a copy of the letter for your file.

If your checks have been lost, stolen, or misused, use the chart for contacting the appropriate check verification service. This is necessary to alert these services that your checks could be used fraudulently. It's a precautionary step to help eliminate possible future problems regarding your checks.

Victim Activity Chart (four pages)

Don't be fooled. The chart may look easy, but the recovery process is a long, detailed, and stressful course. If you decide to take on the recovery process yourself, this four-page chart has contact information for agencies, in-cluding lists of who to contact and places for keeping track of names and dates. (See the "Basic Steps if you become a victim" section for an explanation of why these steps are important).

If you have a recovery service that will handle all your recovery tasks, you can use this chart to confirm each stage of the process. (See "Monitoring and Recovery Services" section for more information).

Sample Letters

Included in this section are three sample dispute letters. While they appear similar, each serves a different purpose. One is to a creditor on a new account, one to a creditor on an existing account, and one to a credit bureau. You will need to include details about your specific issue(s) and any copies of supporting documentation. These are based on sample letters provided by the Federal Trade Commission and are available on line at *consumer.gov/idtheft*.

If you have a recovery service, they will most likely take care of these letters for you. If you are using a recovery assistance service, you may want to have them review the letters before you send them.

Who Else Is You?
How to reduce your risk of becoming an identity theft victim.

Monthly Monitoring Worksheet

Account Type	Acct Name	Jan	Feb	Mar	Apr	May	Jun	Jul	Aug	Sep	Oct	Nov	Dec
Checking													
Checking													
Savings													
Savings													
Investment													
Investment													
Mortgage													
Home Equity													
Car Loan													
Car Loan													
Insurance													
Cell Phone													
Credit Card													
Credit Card													
Credit Card													
Credit Card													
Credit Card													

Annual Monitoring Worksheet

Bureau	Phone	Date Ordered	Date Received	Comments
Equifax	800-525-6285	January		
Experian	888-397-3742	April		
TransUnion	800-680-7289	September		
Social Security Administration	800-772-1213	Mine		Annual Statements are usually sent out 3 months prior to your birth date
Social Security Administration	800-772-1213	Spouse		
Social Security Administration	800-772-1213	Kids		
Medical Information Bureau	612-426-3660			
Local Department of Motor Vehicles				

Who Else Is You?
How to reduce your risk of becoming an identity theft victim.

Suspect Account List

List all accounts you in which you suspect unauthorized activity

	Type of Account	Financial Institution	Telephone	Date of Activity	Comments
1					
2					
3					
4					
5					
6					
7					
8					
9					
10					
11					
12					
13					
14					
15					

Financial Institution Alert Worksheet

	Type of Account	Financial Institution	Telephone	Date of Activity	Comments
1					
2					
3					
4					
5					
6					
7					
8					
9					
10					
11					
12					
13					
14					
15					

Check Verification Services

If your checks have been stolen or misused notify the appropriate service

Verification Service	Phone	Date Contacted	Contact Person	Comments
TeleCheck	800-710-9898			
Certegy Inc,	800-437-5120			
International Check Services	800-631-9656			

Victim Activity Worksheet   1 of 4

Order Copies of your credit reports Tell the bureau you are a victim of identity theft and they should send you a free report, even if you have already received your free annual report.

Bureau	Telephone	Date Contacted	Contact Person	Comments
Equifax	800-525-6285			
Experian	888-397-3742			
TransUnion	800-680-7289			

Place Fraud Alerts

Bureau	Telephone	Date Contacted	Contact Person	Comments
Equifax	800-525-6285			
Experian	888-397-3742			
TransUnion	800-680-7289			

Submit A Victims Statement

Bureau	Telephone	Date Contacted	Contact Person	Comments
Equifax	800-525-6285			
Experian	888-397-3742			
TransUnion	800-680-7289			

Victim Activity Worksheet   Page 2 of 4

	Telephone	Contact Date	Contact Name	Comments
File a report with the Federal Trade Commission				
Identity Theft Hotline	877-ID-THEFT			
By Mail	Identity Theft Clearing House 600 Pennsylvania Ave N.W. Washington DC 20580			
Online	www.consumer.gov/idtheft			
Contact Law Enforcement Authorities				
Local Law Enforcement Office				
Criminal Violations Contact:				
Law Enforcement The Office that originally arrested your imposter				
District Attorney Where the crime took place				
State Department of Motor Vehicles (DMV)				

Victim Activity Worksheet   Page 3 of 4

Examine credit report for fraudulent accounts or activity, Inquiries, or any other suspicious activity.

Activity	Credit Bureau	Date	Company	Comments
Fraudulent Accounts				
Unauthorized Usage				
Inquiries Made				
Other				

Victim Activity Worksheet   Page 4 of 4

Identity Theft Affidavit

Complete an affidavit for each account.

Account	Date	Witnesses	Comments

Sample Dispute Letter
For A New Account

Date

Your Name
Your Address
Your City, State, Zip Code

Name of Creditor
Fraud Department
Address
City, State, Zip Code

Dear Sir or Madam:

I am writing to dispute an account opened fraudulently in my name. I am a victim of identity theft, and I did not open account number **[insert number of fraudulent account]**. I am not responsible for any charges made to this account.

Enclosed are copies of **[insert description of any enclosed information, such as the police report, ID Theft Affidavit, Request for Fraudulent Account Information forms]** supporting my position. I am also requesting copies of any documentation, such as applications and transaction records, showing the transactions on this **[these]** fraudulent account**(s)**.

Sincerely
Your Name

Enclosures: **[List all that you are enclosing with this letter].**

Federal Trade Commission *consumer.gov/idtheft*

Sample Dispute Letter
On An Existing Account

Date

Your Name
Your Address
Your City, State, Zip Code

Name of Creditor
Billing Inquires
Address
City, State, Zip Code

Dear Sir or Madam:

I am writing to dispute a fraudulent **[charge or debit]** attributed to my account in the amount of $_____. I am a victim of identity theft, and I did not make this **[charge or debit]**. I am requesting that the **[charge be removed or the debit reinstated]**, that any finance and other charges related to the fraudulent amount be credited as well, and that I receive an accurate statement.

Enclosed are copies of **[insert description of any enclosed information, such as the police reports]** supporting my position. Please investigate this matter and correct the fraudulent **[charge or debit]** as soon as possible.

Sincerely
Your Name

Enclosures: **[List all that you are enclosing with this letter]**.

Federal Trade Commission *consumer.gov/idtheft*

Sample Dispute Letter
To A Credit Bureau

Date

Your Name
Your Address
Your City, State, Zip Code

[Insert one of the credit bureaus information here]
Address
City, State, Zip Code

Dear Sir or Madam:

I am writing to dispute as fraudulent the following information in my file. The items I dispute are circled on the attached copy of the report I received. **[Identify item(s) disputed by name of source, such as creditors or tax court, and identify the type of item, such as credit account, judgment, etc. Include a copy of your with your SSN or account number circled, and circle the disputed items]**

I am a victim of identity theft and I did not make the charge(s). I am requesting that the item(s) be blocked to correct my credit report.

Enclosed are copies of **[insert description of any enclosed information, such as the police reports]** supporting my position. Please investigate this **[these]** matter(s) and correct the disputed item(s) as soon as possible.

Sincerely.
Your Name

Enclosures: **[List all that you are enclosing with this letter]**.

Federal Trade Commission *consumer.gov/idtheft*

Who Else Is You?
How to reduce your risk of becoming an identity theft victim.

Index

V

Who Else Is You?

How to reduce your risk of becoming an identity theft victim.

Cindy Schroeter Graham

The information concerning identity theft and how we can protection ourselves is vital.

Learn how to become pro-active in protecting your identity and your good name.

Businesses can host an evening or weekend seminar for employees or clients to provide them with the information they need to organize their information and know what to do when it happens to them.

Seminars are available to groups of 50 or more. Seminars are 3 hours and include a workbook. Copies of "Who Else Is You?" may be purchased prior to the seminar at a discount or made available at the seminar. Seminar fees may be waived if purchasing 200 or more books.

To schedule a seminar go to WhoElseIsYou.com to view the seminar calendar or call 970-285-1581

Seminars are great for employees, clients, groups, clubs and communities Everyone needs to know what they can do to help reduce their risk of becoming the next identity theft victim.

Schedule today at whoelseisyou.com or call 970-285-1581

Books make great gifts and premiums!

Financial advisors, Insurance agents, Realtors, Lenders ...
Your clients are already concerned about identity theft.
Now *you* can provide them with the information they want.

Book Order Form (or go online WhoElseIsYou.com)
Who Else Is You?

_____ Total Books @ $19.95 each.......... $_____

S & H add $5.00 for first book .... $_____

$3.00 for each additional book.

(Sent to the same address).........$_____

Shipped to Colorado add 2.9% Tax $_____

(ALLOW 2 TO 4 WEEKS FOR SHIPPING)   Total $_____

Visa / MasterCard / American Express   Check # _____

Card Number_____

Exp. date ____/____Signature_____

Print Name_____

Address_____

City_____State_____ Zip_____

Email_____

Telephone _____

Ship to: _____

Address_____

City_____State_____Zip_____

Send order form to: Who Else Is You? PO Box 726, Parachute CO 81635

Or Fax: 970-285-1581

Email: WhoElseIsYou@EasyAs123.biz

Special "business personalization" is available on corporate orders of 500 or more.